THE INSTANT RAMEN BAR BLUEPRINT

Building Your Dream Bowl and Business

Kathryn Carter

ChefKatBooks

Copyright © 2024 Kathryn Carter

All rights reserved

The characters and events portrayed in this book are fictitious. Any similarity to real persons, living or dead, is coincidental and not intended by the author.

No part of this book may be reproduced, or stored in a retrieval system, or transmitted in any form or by any means, electronic, mechanical, photocopying, recording, or otherwise, without express written permission of the publisher.

Cover design by: ChefKatBooks
Printed in the United States of America

To you, the dreamer holding this book in your hands, with visions of a steaming bowl of ramen and the vibrant hum of a bustling restaurant filling your heart. This is for your courage to dream, to take that first step, and to chase a life built on passion and flavor. May this book guide you, inspire you, and remind you that what you're creating isn't just a restaurant—it's a space where memories are made, stories are shared, and people come to feel at home. I believe in you and the incredible journey you're about to begin.

To my loving family—my husband and my two beautiful children—thank you for being the foundation of everything I do. Your unwavering love, support, and patience have given me the strength to chase my dreams and help others chase theirs. You are my greatest inspiration and my truest joy.

To every chef, food lover, and entrepreneur who dares to create something extraordinary in the world, this book is also for you. For the countless hours you've spent in kitchens, for the mistakes that taught you resilience, and for the moments when your hard work brought smiles to others—you are the heartbeat of this industry.

Finally, to the power of food itself, for its ability to nourish, to connect, and to bring people together in ways words never could. Let's keep cooking, creating, and sharing love—one bowl, one dish, and one dream at a time.

With gratitude and hope,
Kathryn Carter

"Every ramen bar begins as a dream—a small spark of love for food and the people it brings together. This book is for the ones daring to turn that dream into a reality, one bowl, one story, one connection at a time." – Chef Kathryn Carter

PROLOGUE

"A bowl of ramen is never just a meal; it's a story told in broth, noodles, and love. Every slurp is a connection, a memory, a moment shared." - Chef Kat after far to many drinks one late late night.

You're standing outside a tiny ramen shop, the kind you'd almost walk past if it weren't for the smell. That smell—the rich, savory aroma of broth simmering for hours, the faint char of pork belly sizzling, the unmistakable warmth of comfort in a bowl. You're drawn in without thinking, stepping through the door into a space that feels alive. The air is thick with steam, the clatter of bowls and chopsticks, the hum of conversation that rises and falls like waves. You take a seat, glancing at the handwritten menu on the wall, but you don't need to read it. You know why you're here.

A bowl is placed in front of you, the steam rising in swirls. The broth is deep and golden, the noodles perfectly coiled, the toppings arranged like a small work of art. You lift the chopsticks, take a bite, and everything stops. The flavors hit you all at once—rich, layered, and somehow familiar, like they've been waiting for you. You sit back, holding the warmth of the bowl in your hands, and something stirs inside you. It's more than satisfaction. It's inspiration.

That moment—that feeling—is where this book begins. Maybe you've had it yourself, sitting in a ramen bar or standing over your own stove, tasting the broth you've been perfecting. It's the moment when you realize ramen isn't just food. It's an experience, a connection, a story in every bite. And maybe, just maybe, it's the beginning of something bigger.

This book is about that spark. It's about taking that moment of inspiration and turning it into a reality—a space that feels alive, where people gather, eat, and leave a little better than when they came. Whether you're dreaming of opening your first ramen bar or just starting to imagine what it might look like, you're here for a reason. You have a story to tell, and I'm here to help you tell it.

So let's begin. One bowl, one dream, one step at a time. This is your journey, and I promise, it's going to be worth it.

THE INSTANT RAMEN BAR BLUEPRINT

Contents
Introduction
Part 1: Dreaming Big, Starting Small
  Ch. 1. The Ramen Spark
  Ch. 2. Broth, Sweat, and Tears
  Ch. 3. The Art and Hustle of Ramen
  Ch. 4. How to Boil Bones and Build Empires
  Ramen Bar Journey Break! 1
  Ch. 5. The Leap
Part 2: Building the Foundation
  Ch. 6. Location, Location, Ramen
  Ch. 7. Designing the Dream
  Ch. 8. Broth and Brand
  Ramen Bar Journey Break! 2
  Ch. 9. The Salt Sourcing Secrets
  Ch.10. Starting the Fire of Success
Part 3: The Art of Operations
  Ch. 11. Blood, Broth, and Balance

Ch. 12. Menu Mastery
Ch. 13. Service with a Slurp
Ch. 14. Tech & Tables
Ch. 15. Daily Grind, Daily Gains

Part 4: Growing Your Bowl
Ch. 16. Ramen Marketing 101
Ramen Bar Journey Break! 3
Ch. 17. Beyond the Bowl
Ch. 18. Ramen Reputation
Ch. 19. Branching Out
Ch. 20. Thriving Through Trends

Part 5: Sustaining the Dream
Ch. 21. Weathering the Storm
Ch. 22. Feedback Fuels Growth
Ch. 23. The Ramen Legacy
Ch. 24. Personal Growth Through Ramen
Ch. 25. Your Bowl, Your Legacy
Free Recipes You May Enjoy!
Spicy Miso Curry Ramen
Ruffle Shoyu Ramen
Vegan Coconut Lemongrass Ramen
Smoky Tonkotsu Ramen
Kimchi and Butter Corn Ramen
Email Listing

INTRODUCTION

Imagine it. The hum of conversation drifting through the air, the comforting clatter of chopsticks against bowls, the rich aroma of simmering broth wafting up and wrapping itself around your senses like a warm blanket on a chilly night. This could be your restaurant. Your dream. A ramen bar that feels like a home away from home for everyone who steps inside. It's not just about the food; it's about the experience—a space where people come to nourish their bodies, soothe their souls, and leave just a little bit happier than when they arrived. You might be thinking, "How do I get there? Where do I even start?" That's the million-dollar question. You've had this vision in your head for a while now, a quiet dream that grew louder every time you tried a bowl of ramen that didn't quite hit the mark or when you found yourself daydreaming about the kind of place you'd want to run. A place where the broth is always rich, the noodles are always perfect, and the vibe is always welcoming. You're not just chasing the idea of owning a restaurant; you're chasing the chance to create something meaningful, yours. Let's not sugarcoat it—this journey isn't easy. Starting a restaurant, especially a ramen bar, is like jumping into the deep end of a pool when you're still learning how to swim. There will be insurmountable challenges, days where you'll wonder if you've made a colossal mistake, and moments where you'll want to throw your hands up and walk away. But there will also be triumphs that make every effort worth it. The first customer who tells you this is the best bowl of ramen they've ever had. The regulars start to feel like family. You'll feel pride when you look around and realize, "I built this. This is mine." You don't have to have all the answers right now. In fact, you don't need to have any of them. It would be best if you had needed a spark—a reason to believe in yourself and your dream. Let's take a moment to find that spark. It's a memory of the first bowl of ramen that made you fall in love with the dish. You remember how the broth hugged the noodles, the complexity of flavors dancing on your tongue, and the comfort it brought you. It's the longing to create a space where you can share that same feeling with others, a place that becomes a part of their lives in the way it's become a part of yours.

Your spark is your why. Hold onto it because it will light the way through the tough times ahead. Every great entrepreneur started somewhere, and often, they started small. You don't need millions of dollars in the bank or years of culinary training to make this happen. It would be best to have determination, a willingness to learn, and a belief that this dream is worth fighting for. That's what this journey is about turning your passion into something real, something tangible, something that will make a difference in your life and the lives of others.

Think about the ramen entrepreneurs who started with nothing but a pot, a stove, and a dream. They weren't born with all the answers, and they didn't have a roadmap handed to them. They figured it out, one small step at a time. They experimented, they failed, they learned, and they grew. The only difference between them and you are that they started. They took the leap. You can, too.

This isn't just about opening a ramen bar; it's about creating something uniquely yours. It's about sharing your vision with the world, about bringing people together over a bowl of something simple yet profound. Ramen isn't just food. It's art. It's culture. It's a story told through flavors, textures, and aromas. When you create a bowl of ramen, you're telling a story. The broth speaks of time and patience, the noodles of craftsmanship, the toppings of creativity. Together, they create an experience more significant than the sum of its parts. That's what you're striving for—to tell your story, share your passion, and create something that matters. So, where do you begin? You start by dreaming big and thinking small. Focus on the trivial things, the foundational pieces that will one day support the weight of your dream. Imagine your perfect bowl of ramen. What does it look like? How does it taste? What makes it unique? Now imagine the space where it's served. Is it a cozy corner shop filled with the scent of simmering broth? Is it a sleek, modern spot with an open kitchen where customers can watch the magic happen? Or it's a food truck that brings ramen to people wherever they are, sharing joy one bowl at a time. This is your canvas. Paint it however you like.

Once you've envisioned your dream, it's time to start laying the groundwork. Don't worry about the big picture just yet. Focus on the small steps that will get you there. What's your niche? Will you serve traditional ramen that honors its Japanese roots, or will you put your own spin on it with bold, unexpected flavors? What will set you apart from the countless other ramen spots out there? Your unique selling point, your secret sauce, is what will make people choose you over anyone else.

The journey ahead will require you to dig deep and push yourself in ways you never have before. You'll need to learn about the intricacies of ramen—how to make a rich and complex broth, how to craft noodles with the perfect bite, and how to balance toppings for flavor and presentation. You'll need to understand the ins and outs of running a business, from budgeting and marketing to hiring and training. It might feel overwhelming now, but remember, you're not alone. There are resources, mentors, and even this guide to help you every step of the way.

As we dive into this journey together, remember that success doesn't happen overnight. It results from countless small victories, each building on the last. There will be days when you feel like giving up, but those are when it's most important to keep going. You're stronger than you think and capable of more than you realize. With each challenge you overcome, you'll grow closer to your dream, closer to the moment when you'll stand in your own ramen bar and know that every struggle is worth it. So, let's get started. Let's take this dream off yours and turn it into something tangible. Let's figure out what makes your ramen special, your vision unique, and how to bring it to life. As we move forward, I want you to keep picturing that first bowl of ramen you'll serve in your restaurant. Picture the look on your customers' faces as they take their first bite, the way their eyes light up when they realize this isn't just a meal—it's an experience. That's what you're working toward. That's your goal. Now that you've planted the seed of your dream, it's time to nurture it. In the next chapter, we'll look at how to turn your passion for ramen into a viable business idea. Together, we'll explore how to define your niche, identify your unique selling point, and start shaping the concept that will become your ramen bar someday. Let's take that first step toward making your dream a reality.

PART 1: DREAMING BIG, STARTING SMALL

The Ramen Spark

You're sitting in a bustling ramen bar. The air hums with energy, the sound of conversations and laughter mixing with the clink of chopsticks against ceramic bowls. A rich aroma hangs in the air, earthy and comforting, like a hug in edible form. You take a sip of the broth, and it's like the world outside fades away. In that moment, everything just feels right. That's the power of ramen. It's not just food—it's an experience, a moment of connection, a piece of art in a bowl. That's why ramen is such a brilliant venture to dive into. It's universal yet personal, steeped in tradition yet endlessly adaptable. Everyone loves ramen, whether it's a late-night comfort meal, a quick bite during a busy day, or a culinary adventure in a cozy shop. There's something magical about it, isn't there? And you're here because you're not content with just enjoying it. You want to create it. You want to share that magic with others. You're dreaming of your ramen bar—not just any place, but one that will have people lining up out the door, eager to taste the love and passion you pour into every bowl. You're thinking, "This is a crazy idea. I don't know the first thing about running a restaurant." That's okay. Nobody starts with all the answers. Even the most successful ramen entrepreneurs had no clue what they were doing at the beginning. Take someone like Hana Suzuki, for example. She's not a household name, but in her city, she's a ramen legend. Hana's story didn't start in a fancy culinary school or a high-end kitchen. It started in her grandmother's tiny kitchen in Kyoto, where she learned to make broth from scratch, one painstaking batch at a time.

Hana didn't plan to open a ramen shop. She moved to New York for a corporate job, climbing the ladder but feeling more drained with every promotion. One frigid winter evening, homesick and exhausted, she found herself craving the ramen her grandmother used to make. She spent the whole night recreating it in her tiny apartment kitchen, and when she finally tasted it, she felt like she was home again. That was her spark. She started hosting ramen nights for friends, who couldn't stop raving about her bowls. They pushed her to take the leap, and after months of hesitation, she finally did.

It wasn't smooth sailing for Hana. She had to scrape together savings, learn how to run a business, and deal with more setbacks than she could count. But she kept going, fueled by that memory of her grandmother's kitchen and the joy her ramen brought to others. Today, her ramen bar is packed every night, and she's known for combining traditional techniques with innovative flavors that keep people coming back for more.

You might not have a story exactly like Hana's, but you have your own spark. Something brought you here. It was a perfect bowl of ramen you tasted once, the kind you still dream about. It's the challenge of creating something with your own hands, something that's more than just food. It's the dream of being your own boss, of building a place where people can gather and connect. Whatever it is, hold onto it. That's your fuel. Ramen is the perfect business venture because it speaks to people on a deeper level. It's not just a meal—it's comfort, nostalgia, adventure, all rolled into one. You can make it as traditional or as creative as you want. You can tell a story with every bowl, whether it's a homage to your favorite flavors or a daring twist that no one's ever seen before. And the best part? Ramen isn't tied to a specific type of customer. It's for everyone. It can be a high-end dining experience or a simple, affordable comfort food. The possibilities are endless, and that means your potential as a ramen entrepreneur is limitless too.

Think about the kind of ramen bar you want to create. Is it a cozy, intimate space where people can escape the chaos of their day? Is it a vibrant, trendy spot where friends gather to share tasty food and laughter? Is it a bold food truck that brings ramen to people wherever they are? Whatever vision you have, it's possible. You just need to start building it, one step at a time. Let me introduce you to another friend: Marcus. He's not a chef by trade. He used to be a high school teacher, and he loved it, but he always felt like something was missing. Marcus had a side hobby—cooking ramen. He was obsessed with it. He'd spend his weekends trying to perfect his broth, experimenting with toppings, and hosting ramen nights for friends. They loved it, but he brushed off their compliments, thinking, "This is just a hobby. I'm not a professional."

One day, a friend dared him to set up a stall at a local food festival. Marcus almost backed out a dozen times, but he went through with it. The response was overwhelming. People were lining up, raving about his ramen, asking where his restaurant was. That festival changed everything for him. It gave him the confidence to start small, hosting pop-ups and eventually opening his own ramen bar. Today, Marcus's place is a community favorite. He'll tell you that his journey was full of mistakes and learning curves, but he wouldn't trade it for anything. If Hana and Marcus can do it, so can you. They didn't start with fancy degrees or perfect plans. They started with passion, with a spark, with the belief that they could figure it out along the way. That's all you need right now. Don't worry about having everything mapped out. You'll learn as you go. The important thing is to take that first step, no matter how small it is.

As we move forward, we're going to explore how to turn your spark into a flame. We'll dive into the nitty-gritty of building your ramen business, from finding your niche to creating a unique selling point that sets you apart. For now, just hold onto that vision of your future ramen bar. Picture it. Hear the laughter, smell the broth, see the joy on your customers' faces. That's what you're working toward. That's what makes this journey worth every ounce of effort. Let's take the next step together.

BROTH, SWEAT, AND TEARS

Let's be honest. Right now, your passion for ramen feels more like a personal love affair than a business idea. You've got the fire—that unshakable belief that ramen isn't just food, it's life—but where do you go from here? How do you transform that deep, undeniable passion into something you can share with the world? That's what this chapter is about. It's time to bridge the gap between your dream and reality by focusing on one crucial step at a time. You already know you love ramen. Now, you must decide what kind of ramen you want to bring to life. This is where your niche comes in. Think about the ramen bars you've visited or seen online. Some focus on tradition, serving bowls that stick to the roots of Japanese ramen culture. Others are bold, fusing global flavors and daring concepts to create something new. Which one feels more like you? Are you drawn to the depth and heritage of authentic ramen, or does the idea of blending unexpected flavors excite you? Whatever path you choose, this decision will shape everything about your business—your recipes, branding, and target audience. Choosing your niche isn't just about your personal taste. It's about understanding your customers. Who are the people you want to serve? What do they crave? You're in a city with a vibrant foodie culture where people are eager to try something innovative. Or you're in a smaller town where there's a hunger for classic, comforting ramen that transports it to the streets of Tokyo. Your niche should balance what excites you and what will resonate with the people you're serving.

Once you've chosen your niche, it's time to hone in on your

unique selling point (USP). This is what will set you apart from the competition. Why should someone choose your ramen bar over the others? It's your commitment to using locally sourced ingredients or your ability to create vegan-friendly ramen that doesn't compromise flavor. It's the atmosphere you make—a space that feels like stepping into another world. Whatever it is, your USP should reflect your values and vision while solving a problem or meeting a need for your customers. Let's revisit Jake Tanaka for a moment. His niche was blending traditional Japanese ramen with flavors from his hometown in California. His USP? Creating a menu where every bowl told a story—from a smoky miso ramen inspired by summer BBQs to a citrusy shio ramen that paid homage to California's lemon groves. Jake's passion for storytelling through food made his ramen bar unforgettable. It wasn't just about the noodles; it was about the experience of tasting something deeply personal and unique. Your USP doesn't have to be complicated. In fact, simplicity often works best. What's the one thing you can do better than anyone else? What's the one aspect of ramen that you're obsessed with perfecting? Lean into that. It might take some trial and error to figure it out, and that's okay. Experiment in your kitchen. Test your ideas with friends and family. Pay attention to what lights people up and what makes them say, "I've never had anything like this before." That's the sweet spot where your passion meets your customer's needs.

Turning your passion into a business idea isn't about reinventing the wheel. It's about finding a way to stand out that feels authentic. Whether it's through your recipes, branding, or how you connect with your community, your ramen bar should feel like an extension of who you are. This is your chance to share a piece of yourself with the world, one bowl at a time. In the next chapter, we'll dive deeper into the building blocks of great ramen—broth, noodles, toppings—and how to balance tradition with creativity. Keep exploring your niche, refining your USP, and dreaming about the kind of ramen bar you want to create. Every decision you make brings you closer to turning your vision into reality.

THE ART AND HUSTLE OF RAMEN

Great ramen starts with a great bowl, and every great bowl has three essential components: broth, noodles, and toppings. These three elements are the holy trinity of ramen, the foundation upon which everything else is built. If you can master these, you're well on your way to creating something extraordinary. This chapter is about breaking those components down, understanding what makes them shine, and finding the balance between authenticity and creativity. Let's start with the broth. The broth is the soul of ramen, the element that ties everything together. It's where the depth of flavor comes from, and it's what keeps people coming back for more. There are countless styles of ramen broth, each with its own unique character. Tonkotsu, rich and creamy, is made by simmering pork bones for hours until the marrow releases its magic. Shoyu, soy-based, has a salty, savory depth that feels like a warm hug. Shio, light and delicate, lets the other ingredients shine. Miso, bold and earthy, is a favorite for its comforting complexity. The key to a great broth is patience. You can't rush it. The flavors need time to develop, to meld together into something greater than the sum of their parts.

Experiment with different broths until you find the one that feels like yours. It's a classic tonkatsu that you've perfected through trial and error. It's a shio broth with a twist infused with the essence of herbs or citrus. Don't be afraid to get creative. Start with the basics, then make it your own. Research recipes, watch videos, and learn from the masters, but remember that your broth should tell your story. It's the foundation of your ramen bar, which will make your customers say, "I've never tasted anything like this." Next, let's talk about noodles. Noodles are more than just a vehicle for the broth. They're an essential part of the experience, bringing texture, bite, and balance to the bowl. The best ramen noodles have a springy, chewy quality that pairs perfectly with the broth, soaking up the flavor without losing their integrity. Different broths call for different noodles. Thin, straight noodles work beautifully with tonkatsu. Thick, wavy noodles are perfect for miso. There's no one-size-fits-all solution. Your noodles should complement your broth, enhancing its flavor and texture rather than overpowering it.

Consider making your own noodles. It's a labor of love, but it gives you complete control over the final product. If that's not feasible, work with a supplier who can provide high-quality noodles that match your vision. Pay attention to details like texture, thickness, and even the way the noodles interact with the broth. These small choices can make a significant difference in the overall experience.

Finally, let's dive into toppings. Toppings are where your creativity can really shine. Traditional ramen toppings include chashu pork, marinated eggs, bamboo shoots, and green onions. These elements are tried and true, and they bring a sense of authenticity to your bowl. But toppings are also an opportunity to think creatively. What unique flavors or textures can you add to make your ramen stand out? It's a drizzle of chili oil for a spicy kick or a sprinkle of sesame seeds for a nutty depth. It's a seasonal vegetable that adds freshness and color. The key is balance. Your toppings should complement the broth and noodles, enhancing the overall experience without stealing the spotlight. Sourcing ingredients is a crucial part of the process. High-quality ingredients are non-negotiable if you want to create ramen that people will rave about. Look for suppliers who can provide fresh, authentic ingredients, whether it's locally sourced vegetables or imported miso. Build relationships with your suppliers. Visit local markets. Explore new ingredients that inspire you. The better your ingredients, the better your ramen. Balancing authenticity with creativity is one of the most rewarding challenges you'll face. You want your ramen to honor its roots while also reflecting your unique vision. Start with the traditional elements, then add your own twist. You infuse your broth with unexpected flavors or experiment with non-traditional toppings. You create vegan ramen that's every bit as satisfying as its meat-based counterpart. Whatever you do, make sure it feels true to you. As you work on perfecting your broth, noodles, and toppings, keep your customers in mind. What will they love? What will surprise and delight them? Test your recipes with friends and family. Pay attention to their feedback. Use their input to refine your approach. The process of creating great ramen is a journey, and every step brings you closer to your vision. In the next chapter, we'll shift our focus to the business side of things, crafting a plan that will turn your passion into a sustainable reality. For now, keep experimenting, refining, and keep dreaming. Every bowl you create is a step closer to the ramen bar you've always imagined.

HOW TO BOIL BONES AND BUILD EMPIRES

Hana's hands were trembling as she stared at the blank sheet of paper in front of her. She had come so far already, from the comforting nights spent replicating her grandmother's ramen in her New York apartment to hosting small ramen pop-ups that drew lines out the door. Those moments fueled her. They gave her confidence in her food and the way it connected with others. Yet here she was, staring at the daunting task of crafting a business plan. This felt different. The stakes felt higher now. It wasn't just about the food anymore; it was about making a dream sustainable, scalable, and real. You might feel like Hana does right now excited but overwhelmed. Putting your dream onto paper can feel like taking something magical and reducing it to black and white text, spreadsheets, and projections. It's not an easy task, but it's a necessary one. A business plan is the bridge between your vision and its reality. It's how you take the passion and artistry of ramen-making and turn it into a functioning, profitable business that stands the test of time.

Hana began by outlining the core of her ramen bar. She wrote about the experience she wanted her customers to have, the flavors she wanted to share, and the stories her food would tell. For her, it wasn't just about the bowls of ramen. It was about recreating that feeling of comfort and connection she had in her grandmother's kitchen. What do you want your ramen bar to be known for? Start with that. Write it down. Describe it as vividly as you can, as if you're painting a picture for someone who's never experienced it before. This is your foundation, your north star that will guide every decision you make.

Next came the harder part—the numbers. Hana wasn't a numbers person, but she knew this step was crucial. She needed to understand what it would take to bring her vision to life financially. She started with the basics: How much would it cost to rent a space? What would she need to spend on equipment, ingredients, permits, and initial marketing? She reached out to other small business owners, read everything she could about restaurant budgeting, and got advice from a local financial advisor who believed in her dream. She learned how to estimate her monthly expenses and how much she would need to charge per bowl of ramen to cover costs and make a profit. Financial forecasting might sound intimidating, but it's a skill you can learn, just like making ramen. Break it down into small, manageable pieces. List out every possible expense you can think of, from major ones like rent and salaries to smaller ones like napkins and chopsticks. Research the going rates for these costs in your area. Talk to people who have done it before. You don't have to figure it all out on your own. There are resources, mentors, and even free tools online to help you build a realistic budget.

Finding mentors was one of the best decisions Hana made during this process. She reached out to a chef she admired who ran a successful noodle shop a few towns over. She asked if she could pick his brain, and to her surprise, he agreed. They met for coffee, and he shared his experiences—the mistakes he made, the lessons he learned, and the advice he wished someone had given him when he was starting out. He even introduced her to a food supplier who gave her a discount on her first bulk order. Don't underestimate the power of asking for help. People are often more willing to share their knowledge than you might think. Look for mentors in your community or online. Join entrepreneur groups, attend workshops, and surround yourself with people who believe in you and your vision. As Hana's business plan started to take shape, she began to feel a sense of clarity and purpose. The numbers were daunting, but they were also empowering. They gave her a roadmap, a way to measure her progress and make informed decisions. More importantly, they turned her dream into something tangible. She could see it now—not just the ramen bar itself, but the steps she needed to take to make it a reality. You'll feel that too. Crafting a business plan is arduous work, but it's also incredibly rewarding. It forces you to think critically about your dream, to identify potential challenges and come up with solutions before they arise. It's your chance to answer the tough questions: What makes your ramen bar different? Who are your customers? How will you reach them? How will you ensure your business stays profitable? Every question you answer brings you closer to your goal.

Hana wasn't just crafting a business plan; she was building her confidence. With each section she completed, she felt more prepared, more capable. She knew she wasn't alone on this journey. She had her mentors, her family, and her community behind her. Most importantly, she had herself—her passion, her determination, and her belief that this dream was worth pursuing. If Hana can do it, so can you. It doesn't matter if you don't have all the answers right now. What matters is that you start. Take it one step at a time. Write down your vision. Crunch the numbers. Reach out for advice. Every small action you take is a step closer to the ramen bar you've been dreaming of. You have everything you need within you to make this happen. In the next chapter, we'll talk about taking that vision and turning it into action—finding the right location, designing your space, and setting the stage for your grand opening. For now, focus on your plan. It's the foundation of everything to come. Keep going, because your dream is worth it.

Ramen Bar Journey Break! 1

You've just finished outlining the business plan for your ramen bar. I know it might feel a little overwhelming right now—so many numbers, so many ideas, and so many details crammed onto those pages. Your vision is starting to take shape, though, isn't it? The outline, the goals, the budgets—it's all there. Maybe it's rough around the edges, and maybe you're staring at parts that make you think, *How am I going to pull this off?* That's okay. It's supposed to feel big. That's how you know you're dreaming the right size. Now I want you to pause, just for a moment. Take a deep breath and look back at what you've already done. This isn't just a plan; it's the first draft of your future ramen bar. You've put your heart into words. You've scribbled down the kind of place you want to create, the kind of experience you want to share, and the goals that are driving you forward. That's huge. Not everyone gets this far, you know. Most people get stuck somewhere between *"I have an idea"* and *"I'll do it someday."* You didn't let yourself stop there, and that's worth celebrating. Here's what I want you to do now. Close your eyes and picture it—your ramen bar, the way you want it to look on opening day. You're standing just outside the door, and for the first time, you see it for real. The sign above the door reflects everything you've worked for. What does it say? What colors and designs are you looking at? Picture it clearly. Let the letters mean something to you.

Now step inside. What does the space feel like? Is the light warm and soft, or is there a more modern, edgy glow? You hear the gentle hum of conversation, the clatter of bowls, the sound of noodles being slurped with satisfaction. The air smells like rich broth simmering, warm and savory and inviting. What's the first thing your customers see when they walk in? A cozy counter with a view of the kitchen? A welcoming dining room that feels like home? This is your space. You've created it.

Next, I want you to think about the bowl of ramen that started it all. Maybe it's the ramen that made you fall in love with the dish. Maybe it's the recipe you've been perfecting for months, tweaking the broth and adjusting the toppings until it felt *just right*. Picture someone sitting at a table, the steam curling up as they take their first bite. What does their face look like? Are they smiling, closing their eyes as they taste the hours you've poured into that broth? That's why you're doing this—to create moments like that. I know you've been working on your financial goals in this chapter. Let's take a minute to pull those numbers into focus. Yes, the numbers can feel intimidating. Writing down how much you need to get started—rent, equipment, supplies, payroll—makes it all feel so real. But those numbers are just pieces of the puzzle, and they don't have to scare you. Let's make it simple. Write down the *one thing* you absolutely cannot compromise on. Maybe it's the quality of your broth. Maybe it's the ambiance you're dreaming of. That's your anchor—your non-negotiable. Everything else will fit around it.

Now look at your financial goals again, but this time through the eyes of someone who believes in you—because I do, and so will others. How much money do you need to get started? How will you get it? Will you start with a small pop-up to test the waters, or will you pitch your plan to friends, family, or even investors? Take out a notebook, or sit down with your laptop, and write the answers to these questions:

What will it cost to bring your ramen bar to life? Be as specific as you can right now. Break it into categories—rent, equipment, ingredients, staffing. Write it down, no matter how scary it looks.

How will you fund it? Will you use savings, take out a small business loan, or launch a crowdfunding campaign? Maybe a mix of all three?

What are your short-term and long-term financial goals? Do you want to be profitable within six months? A year? How will you get there?

This is where the "how" of your dream starts to take shape. You've already outlined the *what*—your vision, your goals, your menu ideas. Now you're laying the foundation to make it happen. I want you to write everything down, even if it feels messy and uncertain. It's okay if you don't have all the answers yet. The act of writing it out—of giving your ideas a place to live—will help you see where you need to focus next.

When you're done, take a step back. Read through everything you've written so far. Your vision is on the page. Your goals are clearer now. The numbers are there, staring back at you. I know it feels like a lot, but this is where it all begins. You're building something real, something tangible, and something that matters. This is the messy, beautiful part of the journey where everything starts to take shape. Let's take one more moment to dream before we move on. Picture yourself a year from now. You're standing in your ramen bar during a busy evening. Customers are laughing, talking, and savoring the bowls you've created with so much care. Your team is working together like a well-oiled machine, the kitchen humming with energy and precision. Someone catches your eye and gives you a nod of appreciation. Maybe it's a customer, maybe it's your head chef, or maybe it's someone you've mentored along the way. Either way, it's a moment you'll remember forever—the moment you realize you've built something you can be proud of.

You're ready now. Chapter 5 is waiting, and it's all about taking that leap—the first steps to making this dream a reality. You've done the planning. You've built the vision. Now it's time to move forward. You've got this.

THE LEAP

The idea of starting your own ramen bar feels incredible, doesn't it? You can picture the space, smell the broth, hear the clatter of bowls and chopsticks, and see the smiles on your customers' faces. It feels so close you could almost reach out and touch it. Then, as you sit down to take the next step, doubt creeps in. Can you really do this? What if it doesn't work? What if you fail? That voice of doubt is natural, but it doesn't define you. Fear has a way of making everything feel bigger than it is. It's important to remember that those feelings don't mean you're not ready. They mean you care. They mean you want this dream to work so badly that the thought of it not happening feels overwhelming. That's a good thing because it means you're invested.

The first step to overcoming that fear is to face it head-on. Start by acknowledging it. Say to yourself, "Yes, this is scary, and yes, I have doubts, but I also have the passion, the vision, and the determination to see this through." Fear doesn't have to disappear for you to move forward. You just must take the first step despite it. Securing initial funding is often one of the scariest hurdles for aspiring restaurant owners. The thought of asking someone for money or taking on debt might feel daunting. You might wonder how anyone could believe in your vision as much as you do. The truth is passion is contagious. When you genuinely believe in your idea, that belief shines through, and it inspires others to believe in you too.

Start by exploring all the funding options available to you. Maybe it's a small business loan, a crowdfunding campaign, or even asking friends and family for support. Each path comes with its own challenges and rewards. What's important is finding the one that feels right for you. If you're unsure where to begin, consider reaching out to local small business organizations or financial advisors who can guide you through the process. Creating a detailed business plan is your next step. A solid plan doesn't just show potential investors that you're serious; it also gives you a roadmap to follow as you move forward. Include everything from your vision and mission to your financial projections and marketing strategy. Be honest about the challenges you might face and the solutions you've planned for them. The more prepared you are, the more confident you'll feel.

Once you've secured funding, the reality of your dream starts to take shape. It's no longer just an idea in your head; it's something tangible. You've found the perfect space for your ramen bar, or maybe you're still searching. Either way, those first steps bring you closer to your goal. This is where the excitement starts to outweigh the fear. Every decision you make, every small victory, builds momentum. You'll have moments where the challenges feel overwhelming. A supplier falls through, and you're left scrambling to find a replacement before your timeline gets derailed. Perhaps the numbers in your budget don't add up the way you expected, forcing you to rethink your financial strategy. These moments will test your resolve, but they don't have to stop you. Challenges are part of the process, and every entrepreneur faces them in some form. The key is learning to adapt, to see obstacles not as roadblocks but as opportunities to grow and refine your vision.

PART 2: BUILDING THE FOUNDATION

Location, Location, Ramen

Choosing the best location for your ramen bar isn't just about picking a spot where people will pass by—it's about creating an experience that customers want to come back to. It's about finding a place that fits your vision, your budget, and your customers' needs. The location you choose will shape the story of your restaurant, from the kind of people who walk through the door to the ambiance you create inside. It's one of the biggest decisions you'll make as a business owner, and it sets the foundation for everything else. When you think about where to set up your ramen bar, you're not just picking a random spot on the map. You're choosing a community to serve, a setting to call home, and a stage where your vision will come to life. You need to ask yourself some important questions: Who are your ideal customers? What kind of vibe do you want to create? What's your budget? Each of these questions will lead you closer to finding the perfect place.

Urban areas offer vibrant, bustling streets filled with potential customers, but they come with a hefty price tag. Rent is often sky-high, and competition can be fierce. On the flip side, urban environments also mean foot traffic, diversity, and a higher likelihood of attracting adventurous eaters. If you're planning to open your ramen bar in a big city, you need to think about what makes your concept stand out. What's going to draw people in when there are a dozen other restaurants just around the corner? Is it your unique take on ramen, your killer branding, or the cozy atmosphere that invites people to linger? Whatever it is, make sure you highlight it. Suburban locations, on the other hand, might offer more affordable rents and a slower pace of life, but they come with their own challenges. Suburban diners tend to prioritize convenience and family-friendly spaces, so you'll need to create a menu and ambiance that appeals to a broader audience. You offer kid-friendly options alongside your signature ramen bowls or create a loyalty program that rewards families who come back week after week. Suburban customers are often more loyal to local businesses, so if you can win them over, you might find yourself with a solid, dependable customer base.

Another option that's becoming increasingly popular is starting with a food truck. Food trucks allow you to test your concept with lower overhead costs and greater flexibility. You can move to where the crowds are, set up shop at festivals and events, and build your brand before committing to a permanent location. Food trucks also let you focus on a streamlined menu, perfecting a few dishes rather than juggling a full kitchen right off the bat. If you're considering a food truck, think about where you'll park, what permits you'll need, and how you'll build a following. Social media becomes your best friend when your location changes daily. Once you've narrowed down the type of location you're aiming for, it's time to dig into the details. One of the first things to consider is visibility. Are people going to see your ramen bar as they walk or drive by? A spot on a busy street corner with lots of foot traffic can make a stark difference, especially if you're relying on people discovering your restaurant for the first time. However, visibility isn't just about being on a main road. Sometimes, a cozy spot tucked away in a neighborhood can become a hidden gem if you market it well. Parking is another crucial factor. No matter how great your ramen is, customers won't want to come if it's impossible to find a parking spot. If you're in an urban area, think about whether there's public transportation nearby or if you can partner with a local garage to offer discounted parking. For suburban spots, make sure there's plenty of parking available for families and groups.

Negotiating leases and permits is where things can get tricky, but it's also where you have the chance to set yourself up for success. When you're looking at lease agreements, don't be afraid to ask questions and negotiate terms. You might be able to get a few months of rent-free time to set up your space or negotiate a clause that protects you if the property owner decides to sell. Work with a lawyer who has experience in commercial leases to make sure everything is in order. It's worth the investment to avoid costly surprises down the road. Permits are another piece of the puzzle. Every city and county have its own rules, so do your research to find out what you'll need. This might include health permits, business licenses, and inspections for fire safety. It can be a tedious process, but staying organized will save you headaches later. Keep a checklist of everything you need and tackle it step by step. As you start to picture your ramen bar in its new home, think about how the space itself can work for you. If you're designing a cozy, intimate spot, look for smaller spaces with character—exposed brick walls, big windows, or quirky layouts that give your restaurant personality. If you're going for a sleek, modern vibe, think about how you can create clean lines and a minimalist feel. The space you choose will influence your brand, so make sure it aligns with the story you want to tell.

Location is more than just a physical space. It's about creating a connection between your ramen bar and the people who walk through the door. It's about building a community, becoming part of the neighborhood, and creating a space where people feel welcome. No matter where you set up shop, remember that your ramen bar is more than just a place to eat. It's a destination, a gathering spot, and a reflection of your passion. In the next chapter, we'll talk about designing your space to bring your vision to life. From creating an ambiance that reflects your brand to setting up a kitchen that's functional and efficient, we'll dive into the details of turning your location into a true ramen haven. For now, focus on finding the spot that feels right. Trust your instincts, do your research, and imagine the possibilities.

DESIGNING THE DREAM

Creating the perfect space for your ramen bar is about so much more than just arranging tables and chairs. It's about crafting an atmosphere that tells your story, welcomes your customers, and enhances the experience of every bowl you serve. From the moment someone walks through your doors, the ambiance you create will shape how they feel about your restaurant. This chapter is about blending tradition with innovation, maximizing small spaces, and building a kitchen that works as hard as you do. When you think about the ambiance of your ramen bar, picture the feeling you want your customers to have when they sit down. Is it a sense of calm, as if they've stepped into a cozy corner of Japan? Or is it excitement, like they're part of a modern culinary adventure? Japanese decor is a natural starting point for a ramen bar because it ties directly to the roots of the dish. Elements like shoji screens, warm wooden tones, paper lanterns, and subtle floral motifs create an atmosphere that feels authentic and inviting. These touches don't have to be extravagant. Sometimes, a single well-placed detail, like a Sakura painting or a traditional Noren curtain hanging over the doorway, can transform a space.

At the same time, you could add modern twists that reflect your unique personality. You incorporate sleek, industrial elements like exposed metal beams or Edison bulbs to give your ramen bar a contemporary edge. You add bold, colorful murals inspired by street art to create an urban vibe. Whatever you choose, the goal is to balance tradition and innovation in a way that feels natural and cohesive. Think about the story you want to tell through your design choices. Every element, from the lighting to the furniture, should contribute to that story. Small spaces are often the reality for new restaurants, especially in urban areas. That doesn't mean you have to sacrifice style or functionality. In fact, small spaces can be an advantage if you approach them creatively. The key is to make every square foot count. Start by considering how your layout affects the flow of your restaurant. Customers should be able to move comfortably from the entrance to their seats, and servers should have clear paths to and from the kitchen. Avoid cluttering your space with unnecessary furniture or decorations that make it feel cramped. Instead, focus on creating an open, airy environment, even in tight quarters.

One way to maximize a small space is by using multi-functional furniture. Tables that can be pushed together for larger groups or stools that double as storage solutions can make an enormous difference. Wall-mounted shelves or hooks can free up valuable floor space while adding character to your decor. Mirrors are another trick for making a small space feel larger. Strategically placed, they reflect light and create the illusion of depth, giving your ramen bar a more spacious feel. Lighting is another powerful tool for setting the tone of your ramen bar. Soft, warm lighting creates a cozy and intimate atmosphere, while brighter, cooler lighting can energize a more modern, fast-paced space. Consider using adjustable lighting so you can change the mood depending on the time of day. For instance, softer lighting during dinner service can make your restaurant feel more relaxed and inviting. When it comes to the kitchen, functionality is king. A well-organized, efficient kitchen is the backbone of any successful restaurant, and it's especially important for a ramen bar, where speed and consistency are key. Start by thinking about your menu and how your kitchen needs to function to support it. Do you need separate stations for broth preparation, noodle cooking, and topping assembly? How much refrigeration space will you need for fresh ingredients? Answering these questions will help you design a kitchen layout that works for your specific needs.

Even in a small kitchen, there are ways to optimize your workflow. Arrange your equipment and prep stations in a logical order that minimizes unnecessary movement. For example, placing your noodle cooker next to your broth station can save precious seconds during service. Invest in high-quality, durable equipment that can handle the demands of a busy kitchen. It might be tempting to cut costs here, but reliable equipment will save you money eventually by reducing downtime and maintenance costs. Storage is another critical consideration for your kitchen. In a ramen bar, you'll need to keep a variety of ingredients on hand, from fresh vegetables and meats to dry goods like noodles and spices. Make use of vertical space with shelves and racks to maximize your storage capacity without sacrificing accessibility. Label everything clearly so your team can find what they need quickly, even during the busiest shifts.

Cleanliness is non-negotiable in any kitchen, but it's especially important in the tight quarters of a ramen bar. Design your kitchen with easy cleaning in mind. Smooth, non-porous surfaces and stainless-steel appliances are easy to wipe down and sanitize. Make sure there's enough space between equipment and walls to allow for thorough cleaning. A clean kitchen isn't just about passing inspections; it's about creating a safe and efficient environment for your team to work in. As you design your ramen bar, remember that every detail matters. The ambiance, the layout, and the kitchen all work together to create an experience that your customers will remember. Picture someone walking into your restaurant for the first time. What do they see, hear, and feel? How does the space invite them to sit down, relax, and enjoy their meal? These are the moments that build loyalty and keep people coming back. From choosing the perfect name to designing a logo and crafting a story that resonates with your customers, we'll explore how to make your restaurant stand out in a crowded market. For now, focus on bringing your vision to life through thoughtful design. Your space is more than just a restaurant—it's a reflection of your passion and creativity.

BROTH AND BRAND

Branding your ramen bar is about creating something unforgettable. It's more than just a logo or a name—it's the story, the personality, and the promise you make to every customer who walks through your door. Your brand is the soul of your restaurant. It's what makes people choose your ramen bar over the countless other options out there, and it's what keeps them coming back. Hana felt this deeply when she started thinking about how to bring her ramen bar to life. She knew her food was good. Her friends couldn't stop raving about her ramen nights, and even strangers who stumbled upon her pop-up events became repeat customers. Still, she wondered how she could translate that magic into something bigger, something that resonated with people she hadn't even met yet. She realized that her ramen wasn't just about the food—it was about the feelings it evoked. It was about nostalgia, warmth, and the comforting embrace of a bowl of broth on a freezing day. Think about your own story. What led you to this moment, to the decision to open a ramen bar? It was a transformative experience like Hana's, when a bowl of ramen in a small Tokyo shop changed how she thought about food. Or it's the memory of your grandmother's cooking, the way she lovingly prepared meals that brought your family together. Whatever your story is, it's unique to you, and it's the foundation of your brand Hana spent hours reflecting on what her ramen bar would represent. She wanted it to be a tribute to her grandmother's recipes but with a modern twist that reflected her own creativity. She brainstormed names that captured that balance of tradition and innovation. After weeks of jotting down ideas on scraps of paper and tossing them aside, she finally landed on "Kokoro Ramen." The name felt right. "Kokoro" means heart in Japanese, and that's exactly what she wanted her customers to feel when they walked into her restaurant—a sense of heart, of being cared for, and of connection.

Finding the right name for your ramen bar is one of the most exciting parts of building your brand. It's the first impression people will have of your restaurant, so it needs to be memorable and meaningful. Think about what makes your ramen bar unique. Is it your dedication to authentic flavors, your bold and creative twists, or the warm, welcoming atmosphere you create? Let those qualities guide your choice. Once you've chosen a name, it's time to think about your logo. A great logo is simple, versatile, and instantly recognizable. Hana worked with a local designer to create a logo that combined traditional Japanese calligraphy with a modern, minimalist aesthetic. The result was a bold yet elegant design that looked just as striking on a storefront sign as it did on a social media post or a takeout box. Your logo should reflect your brand's personality and be adaptable to different formats and platforms.

Storytelling is another powerful tool for building your brand. People don't just want to eat ramen; they want to feel connected to the story behind it. Hana used social media to share her journey, from her childhood memories of cooking with her grandmother to the challenges and triumphs of starting her own business. She posted behind-the-scenes photos of her recipe testing process, videos of her crafting bowls of ramen, and heartfelt captions about her love for the craft. Her followers became invested in her story, cheering her on every step of the way. Your story is your superpower. Share it authentically and often. Whether it's through social media, your website, or the conversations you have with customers, let people know why you're passionate about ramen and what makes your bar special. This connection builds loyalty and turns first-time visitors into lifelong fans.

Standing out in a crowded market can feel daunting, especially when there are so many ramen bars and restaurants vying for attention. The key is to focus on what makes you different. Hana leaned into her unique selling points—her innovative toppings, her commitment to using locally sourced ingredients, and the intimate, homey vibe of her restaurant. She didn't try to compete with every ramen bar in the city; she focused on being the best version of herself. Think about what sets you apart. It's a signature dish that no one else offers, like a smoky miso ramen inspired by your favorite childhood flavors. It's the experience you create, like a noodle-pulling demonstration at the counter or a cozy library corner where customers can relax with a book while they eat. Whatever it is, lean into it. Highlight it in your marketing, your menu, and your decor. Make it the thing people talk about when they leave your restaurant.

Branding isn't just about attracting customers; it's about creating a sense of identity for yourself and your team. Hana found that having a clear brand vision helped her stay focused and make decisions that aligned with her values. When she faced challenges, like choosing between two suppliers or deciding how to price her menu, she asked herself, "Does this fit with what Kokoro Ramen stands for?" That clarity kept her grounded and confident in her choices. As you build your brand, remember that it's an ongoing process. Your brand will evolve as your business grows, and that's okay. What matters is staying true to your story and your values. The more authentic and consistent you are, the stronger your brand will become. In the next chapter, we'll explore sourcing the ingredients that bring your brand to life. From finding the freshest noodles and broth bases to building relationships with suppliers, we'll dive into the details of creating ramen that's as unforgettable as your story. For now, focus on your brand identity. Let it reflect your passion, your creativity, and your heart.

Ramen Bar Journey Break! 2

You've just finished shaping your brand, and I know how big this feels. You've spent hours—maybe days—choosing the name, the colors, and the story you want to tell. There's a piece of you in everything you've created so far. Maybe it's the way the logo reflects your childhood memories of ramen, or the way the name captures the exact vibe you want your customers to feel when they walk through your door. This isn't just branding—it's the soul of your ramen bar starting to come alive. Take a step back and breathe for a second. I know it's been a lot of work to get here. Building a brand is heavy, and the weight of all those choices can sit on your chest like you've been carrying stones in your pockets. But now it's time to let it settle. You've put so much thought into how the world will see your ramen bar, and you should feel proud. You're not just serving food; you're building a place where people will gather, connect, and feel something. That's no small feat. Now, let's take this work one step further. Imagine someone seeing your ramen bar for the very first time. Maybe they're scrolling through Instagram and see your logo for the first time. Maybe they're walking down the street, and the sign above your door catches their eye. What story does your brand tell them? What's the feeling that hits them immediately—before they've tasted a single bite of your ramen? Is it comfort, adventure, or nostalgia? I want you to write it down. Describe it like you're describing a movie scene: the sign, the first impression, the vibe.

Now picture the inside of your restaurant—the menu they hold in their hands. What's the first thing they notice? Is it simple and clean, highlighting the essentials, or does it tell a deeper story? Maybe there's a little note about where your broth inspiration came from or a small detail about the meaning of your ramen bar's name. Those little touches make all the difference. They tell your customers that this isn't just another meal. It's an experience. You don't have to figure it all out right now, but I want you to sit with this: What small details will make your brand unforgettable? Let's dig into the storytelling piece a little more because that's what's going to set you apart. Every ramen bar has noodles, broth, and toppings. That's a given. What makes yours different is the story you tell through your food, your space, and your presence. Maybe it's your family's recipes. Maybe it's your love of blending Japanese tradition with modern twists. Maybe it's the dream you're chasing—the reason you're building this ramen bar in the first place. I want you to write down your story. Where did this journey start for you? Was it a single bowl of ramen that changed everything? Was it a trip, a memory, or an experience that sparked this idea? Your story is the heartbeat of your brand, and people will connect with it.

Take out a journal, a piece of paper, or open a fresh document on your laptop, and write this:

What's the story behind your ramen bar's name? Does it mean something personal, or does it represent a bigger idea? Write it out in detail—like you're telling a friend why it matters to you.

What kind of feeling do you want your brand to create? When someone steps into your ramen bar or sees your logo, what do you want them to feel? Describe it vividly. Make it real.

What makes your ramen bar different? Maybe it's your creative fusion bowls, your commitment to local ingredients, or the way you're turning ramen night into an experience people can't stop talking about. Write down the details that will make you stand out.

Finally, write the story of your ramen bar—the why behind it all. Why ramen? Why now? Why you? Don't overthink it. Just let it pour out of you, one sentence at a time.

You might not feel like you have all the answers right now, and that's okay. What matters is that you start. This is the part of the journey where you take everything you've been dreaming of and give it shape. It's messy, and it's imperfect, but it's yours. Once you've written it down, take a step back and look at what you've created. You're not just building a business; you're building a story that people will remember.

Now imagine you're sitting down with your future team—your cooks, your servers, the people who will help bring your vision to life. You're handing them the menu for the first time, and you're telling them the story of your brand. This is where it all connects: your name, your space, your menu, and the food itself. It all comes back to the story you're telling. That's how you build something unforgettable. When you're ready, close your notebook or save your document, and let it settle. Your brand exists now. It's out of your head and into the world. That's a powerful step. Next, we're going to talk about sourcing—finding the right ingredients to bring your ramen to life. You've laid the foundation; now it's time to build the flavor. Let's get to work.

THE SALT SOURCING SECRETS

When it comes to ramen, every ingredient matters. From the noodles that carry the broth to the toppings that add texture and depth, each component needs to shine on its own and work harmoniously with the others. Sourcing these ingredients is one of the most critical steps in building your ramen bar. It's not just about finding suppliers—it's about creating a network of partners who share your passion for quality and authenticity while helping you stay within budget. Let's start with the noodles. They're not just a supporting player in ramen; they're the backbone of the dish. The texture, the chew, the way they soak up the broth—it all must be right. Finding the perfect noodles can feel like searching for a needle in a haystack, but it's worth the effort. Many ramen bar owners begin by researching local suppliers specializing in fresh noodles. Fresh noodles often have a better texture and taste compared to pre-packaged ones, and working with a local supplier allows you to customize your order. You want thin, straight noodles for a light shio ramen or thick, curly noodles for a hearty miso bowl. A good supplier can work with you to create noodles that suit your recipes perfectly. If local suppliers aren't an option, there are plenty of high-quality international suppliers who specialize in ramen noodles. The key is to communicate your needs clearly and request samples before committing to a bulk order. Pay attention to how the noodles perform under different conditions—how they hold up in the broth, how long they stay firm, and how they complement your other ingredients. Building a relationship with your supplier is essential. Regular communication and feedback can help you refine your product and ensure consistency over time.

Next, let's talk about broth ingredients. The broth is the heart of ramen, the element that ties everything together. Whether you're making a rich, creamy tonkatsu or a light, delicate shio, the quality of your ingredients will determine the depth and complexity of your flavor. Start by sourcing fresh, high-quality bones for your base. Pork and chicken bones are staples for most broths, and many chefs swear by a mix of the two for a balanced flavor. Local butchers or meat markets can be excellent sources of fresh, affordable bones. Don't be afraid to ask questions about the origin and quality of their products. For other broth ingredients like kombu, dried shiitake mushrooms, and katsuobushi (bonito flakes), specialty Asian markets or online suppliers are often your best bet. These ingredients are essential for creating authentic, umami-rich broths. When sourcing these items, look for suppliers who prioritize quality and freshness. A great kombu, for example, should be thick and slightly pliable, with a rich, salty aroma. Don't settle for inferior products just to save a few dollars. Your customers will taste the difference. Toppings are where you can really highlight your creativity while staying true to the essence of ramen. From tender slices of chashu pork to perfectly cooked marinated eggs, each topping adds its own layer of flavor and texture. When sourcing toppings, balance is key. You want ingredients that are high quality but also cost-effective. For proteins like pork belly or chicken, working with a local butcher or farmer can help you get fresh, sustainable options at a fair price. For vegetables like green onions, bamboo shoots, or seasonal additions, consider partnering with local farmers or farmers' markets. Not only will this give you access to fresh, in-season produce, but it also supports your community and reinforces your commitment to quality.

One of the challenges you'll face is balancing cost, quality, and authenticity. It's tempting to cut corners to save money, especially when you're just starting out, but sacrificing quality can hurt you in the long run. Customers can tell when an ingredient isn't fresh or when a dish lacks authenticity. On the flip side, going overboard on premium ingredients can blow your budget and make it hard to turn a profit. The key is to find a middle ground. Prioritize the ingredients that have the biggest impact on flavor—like your broth base and noodles—and look for creative ways to save on less critical components. For example, you might use locally sourced eggs instead of imported ones for your marinated ajitama or choose a cost-effective cut of pork for your chashu.

Building relationships with your suppliers is just as important as finding the right ingredients. A good supplier isn't just a vendor; they're a partner in your success. Take the time to get to know them, learn about their processes, and communicate your needs clearly. If possible, visit their facilities to see how they operate and build a personal connection. Regularly ordering from the same supplier can lead to better deals, priority access to high-demand items, and more personalized service. Don't be afraid to negotiate terms, especially as your business grows and your orders increase.

International suppliers can be invaluable for specialty items, but they also present challenges. Shipping costs, import regulations, and long lead times can complicate the process, so it's important to plan. Work with suppliers who have experience dealing with international customers and can guide you through logistics. Establishing a strong line of communication is crucial for ensuring that your orders arrive on time and in good condition. One of the best ways to find reliable suppliers is by networking with other restaurant owners and chefs. They've been through the process and can offer valuable insights and recommendations. Attending industry events, joining online forums, and connecting with local culinary communities to build your network. These relationships can open doors to new suppliers, bulk purchasing opportunities, and collaborative partnerships. As you source your ingredients, keep your customers in mind. The choices you make will shape their experience and define your ramen bar's reputation. Are you offering something they can't find anywhere else? Are you staying true to the flavors and traditions they expect? Striking that balance between authenticity and innovation is an art, and it starts with the ingredients you choose. In the next chapter, we'll discuss the final steps of setting up your ramen bar: preparing for a soft launch, testing your recipes, and gathering feedback to refine your offerings. For now, focus on building a sturdy foundation with the best ingredients and suppliers you can find. Your dedication to quality will shine through in every bowl you serve, and your customers will taste the difference.

STARTING THE FIRE OF SUCCESS

You're finally here. You've found the perfect spot for your ramen bar, designed it with care, and sourced the highest-quality ingredients. The dream is no longer just in your head—it's starting to take shape in the real world. Now comes the moment when everything begins to come together: setting up your kitchen and dining space, running those first test services, and preparing to open your doors to the public. This chapter is all about making sure your ramen bar is ready to thrive from day one. Setting up your kitchen is one of the most important steps in this process. Your kitchen isn't just the heart of your restaurant—it's the engine that keeps everything running. Every piece of equipment, every work surface, and every inch of space needs to serve a purpose. Efficiency is key here. You want a kitchen that flows smoothly, where every chef and line cook have what they need within reach and can move without tripping over each other.

Start by thinking about your menu and the tasks that go into each dish. Where will you prepare the broth? Where will you cook the noodles? Where will toppings like chashu pork and marinated eggs be stored and prepped? Each of these tasks should have a dedicated station. Group similar tasks together to minimize movement—broth and noodles in one area, toppings in another, and plating near the pass. This setup not only makes your kitchen more efficient but also reduces the risk of mistakes during service. Invest in equipment that fits your space and your needs. For your broth, a large stockpot or a pressure cooker is essential, depending on the style you're aiming for. A noodle cooker with multiple baskets can speed up service and ensure consistency. Refrigeration is another critical consideration. Make sure you have enough fridge and freezer space to store fresh ingredients without overcrowding. Stainless steel prep tables are durable, easy to clean, and versatile—an absolute must for any professional kitchen.

Cleanliness and organization should be non-negotiable. Install plenty of storage shelves to keep everything organized and within easy reach. Label containers and create a system for inventory management so you always know what you have on hand. This isn't just about passing health inspections; it's about creating a kitchen where your team can work safely and efficiently. Your dining space is just as important as your kitchen. It's the first thing your customers see when they walk through the door, and it sets the tone for their entire experience. Whether you're going for a cozy, traditional vibe or a sleek, modern aesthetic, every detail matters. Think about the layout of your tables and chairs. You want a space that feels inviting and comfortable but also allows for smooth traffic flow. Guests shouldn't feel cramped, and your staff should be able to navigate the dining room easily. Lighting plays a huge role in creating ambiance. Soft, warm lighting can make your ramen bar feel intimate and cozy, while brighter lighting can create a vibrant, energetic atmosphere. Music is another subtle but powerful way to set the mood. Choose a playlist that complements your theme and adds to the overall experience without overwhelming conversation.

Once your kitchen and dining space are set up, it's time to test everything out. Running a pre-opening test service or soft launch is one of the best ways to work out the kinks before you officially open your doors. This is your chance to see how your kitchen functions under real-world conditions, how your staff works together, and how actual customers receive your dishes. Invite friends, family, and trusted community members to these test runs. Let them know you're still fine-tuning things and ask for their honest feedback. Are the noodles perfectly cooked every time? Does the broth hit the right balance of flavors? Is the service efficient and friendly? Pay attention to their reactions, and don't be afraid to ask specific questions. The insights you gather during these test runs are invaluable. Soft launches are also a fantastic way to train your staff and build their confidence. Even if you've hired experienced chefs and servers, working in a new restaurant comes with its own set of challenges. Use these test services to practice communication, refine workflows, and establish a rhythm. Encourage your team to ask questions and share their thoughts—it's better to address any issues now than after your grand opening.

Be prepared for things to go wrong during these test runs. Maybe a piece of equipment breaks down, or an ingredient runs out faster than expected. These moments are frustrating, but they're also learning opportunities. Take notes, adjust, and remind yourself that every challenge you overcome brings you one step closer to success.

Gathering feedback is an ongoing process, not just something you do during the soft launch. After every test service, sit down with your team and discuss what went well and what could be improved. Encourage open, honest communication and create an environment where everyone feels comfortable sharing their thoughts. This feedback loop helps you grow as a leader and ensures that your team feels valued and heard. Once you've completed your test runs and addressed any issues, you'll start to feel a sense of readiness. Your kitchen flows smoothly, your dining space feels welcoming, and your dishes are consistently hitting the mark. The excitement builds as you prepare for your grand opening, knowing that you've done everything you can to set yourself up for success. For now, focus on these final preparations. The stage is set, the fire is lit, and your ramen bar is ready to come to life.

PART 3: THE ART OF OPERATIONS

Blood, Broth, and Balance

The success of your ramen bar isn't just about the bowls you serve; it's about the people who help bring your vision to life every single day. Your staff will be the heart of your restaurant. They're the ones who will greet your customers with a warm smile, keep the kitchen running like clockwork, and make every guest feel like they're part of something special. Building a passionate and reliable team is one of the most important steps in creating a thriving business. The first step in hiring the right people is knowing what you're looking for. Passion is non-negotiable. You need team members who care about what they're doing, whether it's perfecting a bowl of ramen, keeping the dining room spotless, or ensuring every guest has a great experience. Experience can be valuable, but it's not always necessary. Sometimes, the best team members are the ones who bring enthusiasm and a willingness to learn. Skills can be taught, but passion and attitude come from within.

When you're interviewing candidates, look for signs of genuine interest in your restaurant and its mission. Ask them why they want to work at a ramen bar specifically. Do they light up when they talk about food, customer service, or being part of a team? Do they seem eager to contribute and grow with your business? These are the qualities that will set them apart. References can also be a wonderful way to gauge a candidate's reliability and work ethic. Reach out to their previous employers or mentors and ask about their punctuality, attitude, and ability to work under pressure. While no one is perfect, a consistent track record of showing up, working hard, and treating others with respect is a good indicator of a strong team member. Once you've hired your team, the next step is training them to deliver consistency and excellence. Even if your staff has restaurant experience, they must learn your specific processes, recipes, and standards. This is where a thorough training program comes in. It might feel overwhelming to create one from scratch but think of it as an investment in your business. The time and effort you put into training now will pay off eventually.

Start by outlining the key tasks for each role in your restaurant. For kitchen staff, this might include learning how to prepare each component of your ramen, from the broth to the toppings. For servers, it might involve mastering the menu so they can confidently answer customers' questions. Once you've outlined the tasks, create step-by-step guides or checklists that your team can follow. These resources will help them feel confident and ensure consistency in every shift. Hands-on training is just as important as written guides. Shadowing is a wonderful way to teach unfamiliar staff members the ropes. Pair them with an experienced team member who can walk them through the day-to-day operations and provide guidance. Encourage your new hires to ask questions and give them plenty of opportunities to practice. The more comfortable they feel, the better they'll perform when the pressure is on.

Training shouldn't stop after the first few weeks. Ongoing education is essential for maintaining ambitious standards and keeping your team engaged. Host regular workshops or meetings where staff can learn new skills, share feedback, and stay up to date on any changes in the restaurant. For example, you might hold a session on plating techniques or introduce a new menu item and give your team a chance to taste it and learn how to describe it to customers. These moments keep your staff invested in the business and reinforce your commitment to quality. Creating a positive work culture is just as important as hiring and training. Your team will spend long hours together in a fast-paced, high-pressure environment. The way you lead and the atmosphere you create will have a massive impact on their morale and performance. Start by treating your staff with respect and showing that you value their contributions. A simple "thank you" at the end of a busy shift can go a long way.

Communication is the foundation of a strong work culture. Make it clear that your door is always open and that you're willing to listen to their ideas, concerns, and feedback. Act on their suggestions when possible and explain your decisions when you can't. Transparency builds trust and fosters a sense of ownership among your team. Recognizing and rewarding demanding work is another key element of a positive work culture. Celebrate milestones, whether it's a record-breaking sales day, a glowing customer review, or a staff member's birthday. Small gestures like treating your team to a meal or giving them shout-outs during meetings can make them feel appreciated and motivated.

Don't underestimate the importance of creating an environment where your team can have fun and build relationships. Team-building activities, like group outings or friendly competitions, can strengthen bonds and make the workplace more enjoyable. When your staff feels like they're part of a family, they'll be more likely to go above and beyond for each other and your customers. As you build your team and your culture, remember that you're setting the tone for your entire restaurant. Your passion, dedication, and leadership will inspire your staff to bring their best to every shift. The energy you create will ripple out to your customers, making your ramen bar a place people love to visit. In the next chapter, we'll dive into the art of menu mastery—crafting a menu that appeals to diverse customers, seasonal offerings, and strategies for maximizing profitability. For now, focus on building a team that shares your vision and values. Your staff is your greatest asset, and with the right people by your side, there's nothing you can't accomplish.

MENU MASTERY

Your menu isn't just a list of dishes; it's a reflection of your passion, your creativity, and your understanding of your customers. It's the heart of your ramen bar, the thing that will draw people in and keep them coming back. Crafting a menu is about more than just choosing dishes you love—it's about finding a way to connect with a diverse range of customers while staying true to your vision. This chapter is about creating a menu that speaks to everyone who walks through your doors, from first-time visitors to loyal regulars. The first step in crafting your menu is knowing your audience. Think about the community your ramen bar will serve. Are you in a bustling urban area with adventurous foodies eager to try bold new flavors? Or are you in a suburban neighborhood where families are looking for comforting, familiar options? Understanding your customers' preferences will help you design a menu that resonates with them. It doesn't mean you have to compromise your creativity, but it does mean finding a balance between innovation and accessibility.

A diverse menu doesn't mean an overwhelming one. You don't need dozens of options to appeal to a wide range of customers. In fact, too many choices can lead to decision fatigue and slow down your kitchen. Instead, focus on a curated selection of dishes that display your strengths. Start with the basics—your signature ramen bowls. These should be the stars of your menu, the dishes that define your restaurant. Whether it's a rich, creamy tonkotsu or a light, delicate shio, make sure your signature bowls are flawless. Once you've nailed the essentials, think about how you can add variety to your menu without overcomplicating it. Offer different protein options, like pork, chicken, or tofu, to cater to different dietary preferences. Include a vegetarian or vegan ramen that's every bit as satisfying as its meat-based counterparts. Consider adding small plates or appetizers, like gyoza, edamame, or karaage, to complement your ramen and give customers more reasons to linger.

Seasonal offerings are another wonderful way to keep your menu fresh and exciting. Use the changing seasons as an opportunity to introduce limited-time dishes that highlight seasonal ingredients. In the summer, you might offer a chilled ramen with light, refreshing flavors. In the fall, a hearty miso ramen with roasted squash could be a hit. Seasonal specials not only give your regular customers something new to look forward to but also allow you to experiment and test new ideas without committing to permanent menu changes. Specials are also a fantastic way to drive excitement and create a sense of urgency. Limited time offers can encourage customers to visit more frequently, knowing that their favorite dish might not be available next time. Use your specials to display your creativity and push the boundaries of what ramen can be. It's a spicy ramen challenge for adventurous eaters or a fusion bowl that blends Japanese flavors with another cuisine. Whatever it is, make sure it aligns with your brand and adds value to your menu.

Menu engineering is where the art of crafting your menu meets the science of profitability. It's about understanding how each dish contributes to your bottom line and designing your menu to maximize revenue. Start by calculating the food cost for each item on your menu. This includes the cost of every ingredient, from the broth to the toppings, as well as any packaging for takeout orders. Ideally, your food cost percentage should be around 30-35%, leaving enough room for labor, overhead, and profit.

Once you know your food costs, analyze your menu to identify your high-profit and high-popularity items. These are your stars—the dishes that you want to highlight and sell the most. Place these items in prominent positions on your menu, like the top of the page or a featured section. Use descriptive language and enticing photos to draw attention to them. For less profitable or less popular items, consider reworking the recipe, adjusting the price, or removing them altogether. Pricing is another crucial aspect of menu engineering. Your prices need to reflect the quality of your ingredients and the value of the experience you're providing. They also need to cover your costs and leave room for profit. Don't be afraid to charge what your food is worth. Customers are often willing to pay more for dishes that feel special, unique, or handcrafted. At the same time, be mindful of your target market and what they're willing to spend. Striking the right balance takes time and research, but it's worth the effort. Presentation is the final piece of the puzzle. Your menu should be easy to read, visually appealing, and reflective of your brand. Use fonts, colors, and layouts that complement the vibe of your ramen bar. Keep descriptions concise but evocative, giving customers just enough detail to make their mouths water. If you're using photos, make sure they're high-quality and showcase your dishes at their best. A well-designed menu not only enhances the customer experience but also reinforces the perception of quality and professionalism.

Testing your menu is just as important as creating it. Before your grand opening, host tasting events with friends, family, and trusted members of your community. Gather feedback on the flavors, portion sizes, and overall appeal of each dish. Pay attention to what people rave about and what leaves them underwhelmed. Use this feedback to adjust and ensure your menu is the best it can be before it goes live. Once your menu is finalized, don't think of it as set in stone. Your menu should evolve over time, based on customer feedback, seasonal trends, and your own growth as a chef and business owner. Regularly review your sales data to see which dishes are performing well and which ones might need a refresh. Stay open to latest ideas and be willing to adapt to changing tastes and preferences. In the next chapter, we'll explore the art of exceptional customer service—

how to train your team to create memorable experiences, handle challenges with grace, and make every customer feel valued. For now, focus on your menu. It's the heart of your ramen bar, and with the right balance of creativity, variety, and profitability, it will set you apart and keep customers coming back for more.

SERVICE WITH A SLURP

Customer service is the soul of your ramen bar. It's the difference between a one-time visit and a loyal customer who brings their friends and family back time and time again. Exceptional customer service isn't just about solving problems when they arise—it's about creating an experience that makes every customer feel like they're part of something special. It's about making them feel seen, heard, and appreciated from the moment they walk into the moment they leave. Hana learned this firsthand. When she opened her ramen bar, she thought her food would speak for itself. She poured her heart into her recipes, perfecting her broth and noodles until they were exactly right. But as customers started filling her dining room, she realized that great food was only part of the equation. One night, a customer's order came out wrong—she had accidentally been served the spicy miso instead of the shoyu ramen she requested. Hana saw the look of disappointment on the woman's face as she hesitated over her bowl. Instead of brushing it off or leaving it to her server to fix, Hana stepped in personally. She apologized with warmth and sincerity, replaced the order quickly, and even brought out a complimentary dessert to make up for the mistake. That customer not only left happy but wrote a glowing review online, calling out Hana's kindness and attention to detail. It was a turning point for Hana, a moment when she realized that how you treat people matters just as much as what you serve them. Think about the experience you want your customers to have when they walk into your ramen bar. It starts with a warm welcome. Train your staff to greet every guest with genuine enthusiasm, making them feel like they've just walked into a friend's home. A simple smile and a friendly hello can set the tone for the entire meal. Encourage your team to pay attention to the petty things—pulling out a chair for someone, offering to take a group photo, or noticing when a customer looks like they might need help.

Handling complaints and special requests with grace is one of the most challenging but important aspects of customer service. No matter how perfect your systems are, mistakes will happen. A dish isn't as hot as it should be, or a customer didn't realize their ramen came with an ingredient they don't like. When these situations arise, the key is to listen actively and respond with empathy. Teach your staff to use phrases like, "I understand how that could be frustrating," or "Let me make this right for you." Avoid getting defensive or dismissive. Instead, focus on finding a solution that leaves the customer feeling valued and respected. Special requests are another opportunity to go above and beyond. A customer asks for their broth extra spicy, or they need a gluten-free option. While it's not always possible to accommodate every request, making an effort goes a long way. If you can't meet their needs, explain why with honesty and kindness, and suggest an alternative if possible. Hana often found that even when she couldn't fulfill a request exactly as asked, her willingness to try left customers feeling appreciated.

Creating a culture of exceptional customer service starts with your team. It's not enough to tell them to be nice to customers—you need to give them the tools and support they need to succeed. Hana developed a training program that focused not just on the mechanics of service but on the mindset behind it. She held role-playing exercises where staff practiced handling tricky situations, from a customer complaining about a long wait to someone unhappy with their meal. These exercises helped her team feel more confident and prepared, so they could respond calmly and effectively when challenges arose in real life. Hana also made it a point to recognize and reward great customer service. She kept a comment board in the back of the restaurant where she posted positive feedback from customers and added personal notes of encouragement for her team. When a staff member went beyond, she celebrated their efforts during team meetings and occasionally treated them to small perks like gift cards or a free meal. These gestures reinforced the importance of customer service and motivated her team to keep striving for excellence. One of the most important lessons Hana learned was that exceptional customer service isn't just about handling problems—it's about creating moments of delight. It's the server who remembers a regular's favorite order, the chef who comes out to ask how someone liked a new dish, or the manager who surprises a birthday guest with a special treat. These small acts of kindness and attention can turn an ordinary meal into a memorable experience. They build loyalty, foster positive word-of-mouth, and create a community around your ramen bar. As you build your customer service culture, remember that it starts with you. Your attitude and actions set the tone for your entire team. Show your staff what it looks like to go beyond for a customer, and they'll follow your lead. Create an environment where your team feels supported, and they'll be more likely to pass that positivity on to your customers. Your customers are more than just transactions—they're the heart of your business. Treat them with care, and they'll reward you with loyalty and love.

TECH & TABLES

The key to thriving in this environment isn't just hard work and hustle it's learning how to leverage the tools and technology available to you. Technology isn't just something nice to have in your ramen bar. It's your silent partner, the system running behind the scenes to make sure everything flows smoothly. It keeps you organized when the tickets start flooding in, helps you serve more customers without losing your mind, and ensures every bowl leaves the kitchen perfectly. Whether you're dealing with your POS system, online ordering, or managing reservations, the right tools will keep your operation on track. Start with the most important system in your restaurant: your point-of-sale (POS) system. If you're still imagining a cash register and a handwritten ticket for each table, you're going to feel like you've stepped into the future. Modern POS systems are so much more than a way to process payments. They're a hub for your entire operation. They help you track orders, manage inventory, split checks, and gather valuable data about your customers and sales. Choosing the right POS system means understanding what you need and finding a tool that can grow with your business.

When you're running a ramen bar, speed and accuracy are everything. A good POS system allows your servers to take orders quickly and relay them to the kitchen in real-time. That split second matters, especially during peak hours when the line is out the door, and your cooks are juggling ten noodle baskets at once. Your team doesn't have to second-guess an order or waste time running back to double-check details. The POS has it all —seat numbers, special requests, modifier all perfectly clear. If you're offering takeout or delivery, an integrated POS system becomes even more critical. Online orders shouldn't feel like an afterthought. A POS system that syncs with your website or third-party platforms ensures that those orders flow directly into the kitchen, just like dine-in tickets. No scrambling to check an app, no missed orders, and no unhappy customers. It's seamless, and it saves you time and stress. Delivery platforms have become a necessity in the restaurant industry, especially in recent years. People love ramen, but sometimes they don't want to leave their homes to enjoy it. Offering delivery through platforms like DoorDash, Uber Eats, or Grubhub allows you to reach customers who might never set foot in your restaurant. However, delivery can be a double-edged sword. These platforms take a cut of your profits, and it's easy for quality to slip if you're not careful. This is why you need to treat your delivery process with the same care and attention as you dine-in service. Invest in sturdy, high-quality packaging that keeps your ramen intact. Customers are trusting you to give them an experience that's as close as possible to eating in your restaurant. Separate the noodles and broth to prevent sogginess and include clear reheating instructions so they know how to enjoy their ramen the way you intended. Delivery isn't just about convenience it's about showing your customers that you care, even when they're eating at home.

Online ordering for pickup can also be a notable change for your ramen bar. Whether customers are grabbing lunch during a busy workday or taking dinner home for their family, offering a smooth, easy pickup process gives them one more reason to choose you. A good system will allow customers to place orders directly through your website, with options to customize their ramen exactly how they like it. The more friction you remove from the process, the happier your customers will be. Reservations are another piece of the puzzle, especially if you're running a small ramen bar with limited seating. You've probably experienced the frustration of walking into a packed restaurant and being told there's a 45-minute wait. Your customers have too, and you don't want that to be their first impression of your business. Managing reservations efficiently allows you to plan for the flow of customers, maximize your seating, and reduce wait times. If you're not ready to invest in a full reservation platform, even a simple phone or email system can work—just make sure it's organized. Keep track of names, party sizes, and times, and communicate clearly with your team about upcoming reservations. For a more automated approach, platforms like OpenTable or Resy allow customers to book tables online and integrate seamlessly with your POS system. These tools can also send automatic reminders to customers, reducing no-shows and keeping your tables full.

Walk-ins are inevitable, even if you take reservations, and you need a plan for managing them. During peak hours, it's easy for your front-of-house staff to feel overwhelmed as customers pour in. Train your team to greet every walk-in with a warm, friendly welcome and a realistic wait time. If there's a waitlist, make sure it's easy to use and transparent. Digital waitlist tools can send customers a text when their table is ready, giving them the freedom to explore nearby shops or take a stroll instead of standing awkwardly at the door. Peak hours are where your systems and planning will truly be tested. When the rush hits, every part of your operation needs to work together seamlessly. Your kitchen needs to fire orders quickly, your servers need to stay organized, and your front-of-house staff needs to keep the flow of customers moving. Technology helps you streamline this process by eliminating guesswork and reducing the chance for errors.

For your kitchen, this might mean using a kitchen display system (KDS) that syncs with your POS. Instead of relying on printed tickets, your cooks can see orders displayed on a screen, prioritized by time and status. This helps the kitchen stay organized and ensures that nothing gets missed, even during the busiest shifts. For your servers, handheld POS devices can make an enormous difference. Taking orders tableside and sending them directly to the kitchen saves time and minimizes mistakes. Managing peak hours is also about preparation. Train your team to anticipate the rush and stay calm under pressure. Prep as much as possible before the doors open—broth, toppings, noodles, everything should be ready to go. Make sure your staff knows their roles and responsibilities, so there's no confusion when the line is out the door. A well-prepared team is a confident team, and confidence is contagious. At the end of the day, technology is there to make your life easier, not more complicated. The tools you choose should fit seamlessly into your workflow and help you deliver the kind of experience you want for your customers. Whether it's a POS system that keeps orders flowing, a delivery platform that expands your reach, or a reservation system that keeps your tables full, each piece of technology is a building block for your success. In the next chapter, we'll focus on the daily grind of running a ramen bar—how to maintain high standards, handle inventory, and troubleshoot challenges as they arise. For now, take a deep breath and look at the systems you've built. Your restaurant is no longer just an idea or a dream. It's a fully functioning operation, ready to take on the busiest nights and the hungriest customers.

DAILY GRIND, DAILY GAINS

Running a ramen bar isn't just about the excitement of opening night or the satisfaction of hearing customers rave about your food. It's about showing up every single day with the same commitment to quality, consistency, and care. The daily grind can be exhausting, but it's also where the magic happens. It's where you prove to yourself and your customers that your ramen bar isn't a fluke—it's the real deal. This chapter is all about how to maintain lofty standards every day, manage the less glamorous parts of the job like inventory and cleanliness, and handle the challenges that will inevitably come your way. Your customers don't see the hours you put in before the doors open, the late nights spent cleaning up, or the quiet moments when you're troubleshooting a problem no one else notices. All they see is the result: a steaming bowl of ramen that feels perfect, a clean and welcoming dining space, and a team that looks like they have everything under control. That illusion of effortlessness is the result of countless small decisions, made consistently and deliberately. Maintaining ambitious standards is a choice you make every single day, and it starts with setting clear expectations for yourself and your team. Think about the quality you want to deliver with every bowl of ramen. The broth needs to be rich and flavorful; the noodles need to be cooked to perfection, and the toppings need to be fresh and carefully arranged. There's no room for shortcuts. Consistency is what keeps customers coming back, and achieving it requires attention to detail at every step. Your team needs to know that there's no such thing as "good enough."

A slightly overcooked noodle or a lukewarm broth might not seem like a big deal, but to the customer, it's the difference between an unforgettable experience and a disappointing meal. Start each day by setting the tone for your team. Whether it's a quick meeting before service or a moment to check in with each person, make it clear that quality is non-negotiable. Walk through the kitchen to ensure everything is prepped and ready to go. Taste the broth to make sure the flavors are where they need to be. Double-check the freshness of your ingredients. These small rituals create a culture of excellence, where everyone is invested in upholding your standards.

Handling inventory is one of the less glamorous parts of running a restaurant, but it's absolutely essential. You can't serve great food if you don't have the right ingredients on hand, and you can't stay profitable if you're constantly throwing away spoiled or wasted items. Inventory management is about finding the right balance between having enough stock to meet demand and avoiding unnecessary waste. Start by creating a system for tracking your inventory. This doesn't need to be complicated—there are plenty of tools and software that can help you keep everything organized—but it does need to be consistent. Know exactly how much of each ingredient you use on a daily, weekly, and monthly basis. Pay attention to trends in your sales data. If your pork-based tonkotsu ramen is flying out of the kitchen every night, you'll need to order more pork bones to keep up. If a certain topping or side dish isn't selling, adjust your orders accordingly.

Organization is key to keeping your kitchen running smoothly. Label everything clearly, from containers of fresh produce to boxes of noodles. Use the FIFO (first in, first out) method to ensure that older ingredients get used before newer ones, reducing waste and maintaining freshness. Train your staff to keep an eye on inventory levels throughout the day so they can alert you to anything that's running low. A well-organized kitchen doesn't just look better—it functions better, too. Cleanliness is another critical part of maintaining ambitious standards. A clean restaurant isn't just about passing health inspections; it's about creating an environment where customers feel comfortable and safe, and where your team can work efficiently. The truth is customers notice everything. They see the smudges on the windows, the crumbs on the floor, and the spots on the silverware. If they don't trust that your dining room is clean, they won't trust that your kitchen is, either.

Create a daily cleaning checklist that includes both front-of-house and back-of-house tasks. Your dining area should be spotless before every service—tables wiped down, floors swept and mopped, chairs straightened, and menus cleaned. Your kitchen should be just as pristine. Countertops should be sanitized, equipment should be cleaned, and floors should be free of spills and debris. It's not glamorous work, but it's the foundation of a successful restaurant. Health inspections are an inevitable part of running a restaurant, and they can be nerve-wracking if you're not prepared. The best way to handle inspections is to treat every day like inspection day. Always make cleanliness and food safety a priority, not just when you know someone is coming to check. Train your team on proper food handling procedures, like storing ingredients at the correct temperatures and avoiding cross-contamination. Keep detailed records of your cleaning schedules and inventory management. When you run a tight ship, inspections become just another part of the routine. No matter how well you prepare, challenges will come up. Your fryer breaks down in the middle of service, or you run out of a key ingredient because of a supplier issue. Learning to troubleshoot these problems is part of being a restaurant owner. The most important thing is to stay calm and focused. When something goes wrong, take a deep breath and assess the situation. Can you fix the problem immediately, or do you need to improvise? If you run out of an ingredient, can you offer customers an alternative? If equipment fails, do you have a backup plan to keep service going?

Having a plan for these scenarios will save you time

and stress when they happen. Keep spare parts for essential equipment on hand and build relationships with repair technicians who can respond quickly when you need them. Have a backup list of suppliers in case your usual one can't deliver. Train your staff to communicate clearly and work together when challenges arise. The smoother you handle these situations, the more confident your team will feel and the less your customers will notice. The daily grind of running a ramen bar can feel relentless, but it's also where the magic happens. Every day is a chance to improve, to learn, and to prove to yourself that you're capable of making this dream a reality. It's not about perfection it's about showing up, solving problems, and delivering the best experience you can, day after day. The challenging work you put in today will set the stage for the success you'll enjoy tomorrow.

PART 4: GROWING YOUR BOWL

Ramen Marketing 101

You've done the hard work of building your ramen bar. The broth is perfect, the noodles are just the right texture, and the ambiance you've created feels like a warm hug. Now it's time to make sure people know about it. No matter how amazing your ramen bar is, if people don't hear about it, they won't show up. Marketing is your way of telling the world who you are, why your ramen is special, and why they absolutely need to try it. Social media is one of the most powerful tools you have for building a following. It's your chance to show people what makes your ramen bar unique and to connect with them in a way that feels personal and real. Think of it as an extension of your restaurant, a place where you can share your story, your passion, and your personality. Platforms like Instagram, Facebook, and TikTok are perfect for displaying your food, your team, and the energy of your space. Each bowl of ramen you serve is an opportunity to create something visually stunning, something that will make people stop scrolling and say, "I need to go there."

Start by creating content that feels authentic. Share behind-the-scenes moments from your kitchen, your chef carefully plating a bowl of ramen, steam rising from a simmering pot of broth, or the joyful chaos of your team during a busy service. These glimpses into your world make people feel connected to your restaurant and build trust. They'll see the care and passion you put into every detail, and they'll want to be part of it.

Stories are another powerful way to engage with your audience. Use them to share quick updates, like new specials or seasonal ingredients you're excited about. Post polls or Q&A sessions to encourage interaction and get to know your followers better. The more you engage with your audience, the more invested they'll become in your success. Respond to comments, reply to messages, and thank people for sharing photos of their meals at your ramen bar. These small gestures create a sense of community around your brand. Partnering with influencers and food bloggers can amplify your reach. These are people who already have an audience that trusts their recommendations, and a single post or review from them can bring a wave of new customers to your door. When choosing influencers to work with, look for those whose values align with yours. It's not just about the number of followers they have—it's about the connection they have with their audience. A smaller influencer with a highly engaged following can have more impact than someone with a massive but detached audience. When you reach out to influencers, make it personal. Let them know why you admire their work and why you think your ramen bar would be a great fit for their content. Invite them to come in for a meal and experience your restaurant firsthand. Don't just treat it as a transaction; build a relationship. Influencers are storytellers, and if they connect with your story, they'll tell it in a way that resonates with their followers.

Events and promotions are another way to create buzz and get people talking about your ramen bar. Think about what makes your restaurant special and how you can turn that into an event that excites your community. It's a ramen-eating contest, a noodle-pulling demonstration, or a special collaboration with a local brewery. Whatever you choose, make it an experience that people will want to share on social media and tell their friends about. Seasonal promotions are also a wonderful way to keep your menu fresh and give people a reason to visit regularly.

Introduce limited-time dishes that highlight seasonal ingredients or celebrate local traditions. Use these specials as an opportunity to experiment and gather feedback from your customers. If a seasonal dish becomes a hit, consider adding it to your permanent menu. Creating buzz is about more than just getting people through the door. It's about building a community around your ramen bar. Think about ways to involve your customers in your story. Host a naming contest for a new dish or invite your followers to vote on the next seasonal special. These interactive moments make people feel like they're part of your journey, and they'll be more likely to support you because of it.

As you build your marketing strategy, remember that it's not just about attracting new customers—it's about building relationships with the ones you already have. Your regulars are your biggest advocates. They're the ones who will bring their friends, write glowing reviews, and share your posts with their networks. Treat them like the VIPs they are. Offer loyalty rewards, surprise them with a complimentary appetizer, or simply take the time to thank them for their support. When people feel valued, they'll keep coming back. Marketing your ramen bar is an ongoing process. It's about finding the right balance between consistency and creativity, between sharing your story and listening to your customers. There will be times when it feels like you're shouting into the void, but don't give up. Every post, every interaction, and every event are a step toward building the kind of buzz that will make your ramen bar a staple in your community. In the next chapter, we'll explore how to expand your revenue streams and grow your business beyond the walls of your restaurant. From catering to merchandise to meal kits, we'll look at ways to take your brand to the next level. For now, focus on sharing your passion with the world. Your story is unique, your ramen is special, and there are people out there waiting to discover it.

Ramen Bar Journey Break! 3

You've made it through the marketing chapter, and let me tell you—this is where the magic starts to happen. Marketing might seem intimidating at first, like a big, loud arena where everyone's shouting for attention, but you've already done something amazing. You've laid the groundwork. You've started telling your story, building your brand, and sharing what makes your ramen bar unique. That's no small feat. You've figured out what you stand for, who you're serving, and the energy you're putting into the world. Now it's time to focus on the connections that will bring all of this to life. Picture this: it's six months from now, and your ramen bar has a line out the door. Customers are snapping photos of your signature bowl and sharing them on Instagram with hashtags that include your restaurant's name. A local food blogger just raved about your broth—so rich and perfect it made their top-ten list of must-try spots. The buzz is growing, not because you bought ads, but because people can't stop talking about you. That's what great marketing does. It connects your story to the right people. It makes your ramen bar feel like the place to be. So let's do something big. I want you to write down what that vision looks like for you. I'm serious—grab a notebook, a piece of paper, or your laptop. Close your eyes for a moment and imagine your restaurant when everything clicks. What does that buzz feel like? What do people say when they talk about your ramen bar? Are they raving about the perfect noodles? The vibe of your dining room? The way your team makes every guest feel like family? I want you to write it all down, as if it's already happening.

Next, think about the tools you need to get there. Maybe it's Instagram. Maybe it's TikTok, where quick videos of your ramen pouring into bowls go viral because they're just that mesmerizing. Maybe it's your website, where you share your story and post updates about your new specials. I want you to list out every tool you want to use to reach your people. Don't overthink it—just brainstorm. Now let's dream a little bigger. Imagine partnering with someone who can help amplify your voice. Who are the influencers or food bloggers in your area who love ramen? Picture reaching out to them with confidence, inviting them in for a meal that showcases exactly what your ramen bar is all about.

Think about what you'd say in that message. You're not begging for attention; you're sharing something you're proud of. You're inviting them into your story. Write that message. It doesn't have to be perfect, but I want you to feel what it's like to ask for help, to share your vision boldly.

Let's take this vision even further. Imagine throwing a launch event for your ramen bar that has people talking for weeks. Maybe it's a ramen-tasting night, where guests get to try small bowls of your most creative dishes. Maybe it's a soft opening with live music, friends, and food that leaves people saying, "I can't wait to come back here." Who would you invite? Write a list of names. These are your people—your family, your friends, the community members and collaborators who believe in you. Now that you've dreamed about the buzz, the connections, and the excitement, let's come back to where you are right now. Marketing is just about one thing: sharing what you love in a way that makes others love it, too. You don't have to do everything at once. Start small. Choose one platform, one partner, one event idea, and start there. Write down the very next thing you're going to do to get the word out about your ramen bar. Maybe it's posting a photo of your signature bowl online. Maybe it's messaging a blogger to invite them in. Whatever it is, write it down and commit to it. That small step is going to build momentum.

Finally, remember this: marketing doesn't have to feel fake or forced. You're not trying to convince people of something that isn't true. You're sharing something real—something you care about deeply. Every time you post a photo, tell a story, or invite someone to try your food, you're sharing a piece of yourself. That's what people will connect with. You're ready to take this next step. I can feel it. When you put yourself out there, when you show the world what your ramen bar is all about, people are going to notice. They're going to feel that energy, and they're going to want to be part of it. Chapter 17 is waiting, and it's all about expanding your vision beyond the ramen bar itself. But before we get there, take a moment to sit with what you've just written. Your vision is starting to move from dream to reality, and this is where the momentum really kicks in. Let's keep going—you're closer than you think.

BEYOND THE BOWL

As your ramen bar starts to settle into its rhythm, you'll find yourself looking for ways to grow. It's the excitement of reaching new customers, or maybe it's the realization that your dream could become even bigger than you imagined. Expanding your revenue streams isn't just about making more money—it's about creating new ways for people to connect with your brand and keeping your business vibrant and dynamic. This chapter is about exploring those opportunities and finding the ones that resonate with you and your vision. Hana remembers the moment she realized her ramen bar could be more than just a restaurant. She was catering a small birthday party for one of her regular customers a group of about 20 people—and she saw the way her ramen brought everyone together. It wasn't just the food. It was the way people laughed and shared stories over their bowls, the way her ramen became part of their celebration. She realized that her restaurant wasn't just about serving food; it was about creating experiences. That realization opened a universe of possibilities. Catering is one of the most natural ways to expand your revenue streams. Your ramen bar already has the food, the team, and the know-how. Offering catering allows you to bring your ramen to customers who might not make it to your restaurant, whether it's a corporate lunch, a wedding, or a community event. Start small, like Hana did, with a handful of simple packages that display your most popular dishes. Focus on items that travel well and are easy to serve, like broth and noodles packaged separately to ensure they stay fresh.

When Hana started catering, she quickly realized the importance of presentation. She invested in high-quality serving containers and a portable ramen station that allowed her team to assemble bowls on-site. It was a hit—customers loved the experience of watching their ramen come together right in front of them. The attention to detail and the interactive element made her catering service stand out, and word of mouth quickly spread. Merchandise is another way to expand your brand's reach while creating an additional revenue stream. Think about items that reflect the personality of your ramen bar and appeal to your customers. It's a T-shirt with a clever ramen pun, a reusable bowl with your logo, or a set of chopsticks engraved with your restaurant's name. Hana started with simple items, like branded tote bags and mugs, and was surprised by how quickly they sold out. Her customers loved the chance to take a piece of her restaurant home with them. Meal kits have become increasingly popular, offering customers a way to enjoy your ramen at home without sacrificing quality. A well-designed meal kit lets people recreate the magic of your dishes in their own kitchens. It's not just about the food—it's about the experience. Include pre-portioned ingredients, clear instructions, and even a little note from you, sharing a tip or a story about the dish. Hana's meal kits were especially popular during the holidays, when families were looking for fun and unique ways to cook together.

Hosting workshops or cultural events is another way to bring people into your world. Imagine teaching a group of enthusiastic home cooks how to make their own ramen from scratch, guiding them through the process of preparing broth, rolling noodles, and assembling a bowl. Hana started offering ramen workshops once a month, and they quickly became a highlight for her customers. She loved the chance to share her knowledge and passion, and her customers loved getting a behind-the-scenes look at her craft. Cultural events can also help you connect with your community and share the rich history and traditions behind ramen. Hana partnered with a local theater to host a Japanese film night, complete with a special ramen menu inspired by the movies. The event drew a mix of her regular customers and unfamiliar faces, all eager to experience something unique. Collaborations like these are not only fun but also strengthen your ties to your local community. Collaborating with local businesses is another way to expand your reach and create something special. Hana worked with a nearby bakery to create a limited-edition ramen-inspired bread, and with a local brewery to develop a beer that paired perfectly with her miso ramen. These partnerships brought in customers from the bakery and the brewery who might not have discovered her ramen bar otherwise, and they created buzz that extended far beyond her regular audience.

As you explore these opportunities, remember that expansion should always feel authentic to your brand. Don't try to do everything at once or force something that doesn't fit. Start with the ideas that excite you the most and build from there. When Hana began catering, she didn't have a grand plan to add meal kits, merchandise, and workshops all at once. She started with one idea, learned from it, and let the rest evolve naturally. Expanding your revenue streams isn't just about growing your business—it's about finding new ways to share your passion with the world. It's about creating moments that bring people joy, whether they're enjoying your ramen at a wedding, wearing your T-shirt on a lazy weekend, or learning to make their own noodles in your workshop. Each of these moments is an opportunity to deepen your connection with your customers and show them what makes your ramen bar special. Your ramen bar is already something amazing now it's time to see just how far it can go.

RAMEN REPUTATION

Your ramen bar is more than just a place to eat it's an experience. It's a community hub, a comfort zone, a space where people come together over steaming bowls of broth and perfectly cooked noodles. To keep that momentum going, you need to cultivate a formidable reputation. This isn't just about attracting new customers; it's about retaining the ones you already have and turning them into your most loyal advocates. Building your reputation starts with encouraging positive reviews, managing the occasional negative one, and creating loyalty programs that make every customer feel like part of the family. Positive reviews are gold in the restaurant industry. They're the first thing potential customers see when they're deciding whether to visit your ramen bar. A glowing review can mean the difference between an empty table and a packed dining room. The best way to encourage positive reviews is to deliver an exceptional experience every time. Your food needs to be consistent; your service needs to be warm and attentive, and your space needs to feel welcoming. When you go beyond for your customers, they'll naturally want to share their experiences with others. That said, sometimes people need a little nudge to leave a review. This doesn't mean begging for feedback or coming across as desperate. It's about finding organic ways to encourage your customers to share their thoughts. A simple comment from a server "We'd love to hear what you think on Yelp or Google!" can go a long way. You can also include a friendly reminder on your receipts or table tents, inviting guests to leave a review if they enjoyed their meal. Make it easy for them by providing direct links or QR codes that take them straight to your review page.

Responding to reviews is just as important as receiving them. Thanking customers for their positive feedback shows that you value their opinion and appreciate their support. Take the time to personalize your responses when possible, mentioning specific details from their review. This small effort makes a substantial impact, showing potential customers that you genuinely care about your guests' experiences. Managing negative reviews is a skill every restaurant owner needs to master. No matter how hard you try, there will be times when someone isn't satisfied. Their ramen wasn't as hot as they expected, or maybe their server seemed distracted. When you come across a negative review, resist the urge to get defensive. Instead, approach it as an opportunity to learn and improve. Respond with empathy and professionalism, thanking the customer for their feedback and addressing their concerns. If possible, offer to make things right invite them back for another meal or provide a direct way for them to contact you. Handling negative reviews with grace not only helps repair your relationship with that customer but also demonstrates to others that you take feedback seriously and are committed to excellence.

While reviews play a crucial role in shaping your reputation, building loyalty programs is how you keep customers coming back. Loyalty programs aren't just about discounts or free meals they're about making your customers feel valued and appreciated. A good loyalty program rewards repeat visits in a way that feels meaningful and personalized. It's a points system where customers earn rewards for each bowl of ramen they order, or maybe it's a VIP program that gives members early access to new menu items and exclusive events. The key to a successful loyalty program is simplicity. Customers should be able to understand how it works and see the benefits clearly. Digital loyalty programs are especially effective because they're easy to track and manage. Apps or online platforms allow customers to sign up quickly, keep track of their points, and redeem rewards seamlessly. Hana once shared a great idea: giving customers a beautifully designed loyalty card with a small gift on their first visit, like a free topping upgrade or a discount on their next bowl. It's a gesture that says, "We're glad you're here, and we want to see you again." Turning occasional diners into brand ambassadors is the next step in building your reputation. These are the customers who go beyond simply enjoying your food they become champions for your brand, telling their friends and family about your ramen bar and sharing their experiences on social media. To create brand ambassadors, you need to focus on connection. Make every customer feel like they're part of something special.

Start by engaging with your customers both in-person and online. Remember their names, their favorite orders, and the minute details that make them feel seen. If someone always orders the same bowl of spicy miso ramen, have your server mention it when they walk in: "Spicy miso today, right?" These small touches create a sense of familiarity and belonging. Social media is a powerful tool for turning loyal customers into advocates. Encourage them to share their meals with their followers by creating photo-worthy dishes and providing hashtags or geotags for your restaurant. Feature customer photos and stories on your own social media accounts it's a win-win that celebrates your customers while showcasing your brand. Hosting contests or giveaways can also spark excitement and encourage participation. Imagine offering a free meal to the customer who posts the best ramen photo of the week or tagging loyal followers in your posts to thank them for their support. Building a compelling reputation takes time, but every step you take brings you closer to creating a community around your ramen bar. Your reputation is more than just the reviews people leave or the loyalty cards they fill out it's the feeling they have when they think about your restaurant. It's the warmth of your service, the consistency of your food, and the joy they experience every time they visit. For now, focus on building the foundation of your reputation. Each positive review, each loyal customer, and each brand ambassador brings you closer to achieving your vision.

BRANCHING OUT

When you opened your ramen bar, it felt like climbing a mountain. There were so many moving parts, so many days of doubt, and so many victories to celebrate. Now, as you look around, it's working. Your seats are filling up, people know your name, and customers are walking out with smiles on their faces. You're even starting to hear a familiar refrain: "I wish you had a location closer to me!" or "When are you opening another spot?" That little voice in the back of your mind starts to get louder, asking the question you can't ignore anymore when is it time to expand? The thought of opening a second location can be thrilling and terrifying all at once. You're proud of what you've built, and the idea of recreating that success somewhere else is exciting. At the same time, you know how much work it took to get here, and you wonder if you can do it again. Expansion isn't a decision to take lightly. It's not just about doubling your business it's about protecting what you've already built while carefully, thoughtfully growing into something bigger. Knowing when to expand is the first and most key step. It starts with recognizing whether your current location is truly thriving. A packed dining room on a Friday night is great, but is your ramen bar consistently profitable? Look at your numbers. Are you regularly hitting your sales goals? Is your cash flow stable? If you're barely keeping your head above water at your first location, expanding can be risky. Your first location needs to be a well-oiled machine before you even think about opening another one. It needs to operate so smoothly that it can survive and thrive without you being there every moment.

Take a close look at your systems and your team. Do you

have strong processes in place for everything from inventory management to training fresh staff? Can you trust your current team to run the first location while you focus on the second? Many ramen bar owners find that expansion forces them to step back and look at the bigger picture. You'll need to shift from being the heart of your restaurant to being the leader of a growing business. That means empowering your team, delegating responsibilities, and trusting others to uphold the standards you've set. Once you've decided that you're ready to expand, the next question is where to go. Finding the right location is just as important for your second spot as it was for your first. Think about what made your original location successful. Was it the foot traffic? The community? The lack of other ramen options nearby? Use that knowledge to guide your search. You're looking for a location that has the same magic—a place where your ramen bar can fill a need and become a beloved part of the neighborhood. Consider whether you want to stay local or expand to a different city or region. Keeping it local has its advantages. You already know the market, and you may have a built-in customer base excited to visit your new spot. Local expansion can also make it easier to manage both locations, since you won't have to travel far to keep an eye on things. On the other hand, expanding to a new area can help you reach a fresh audience and introduce your brand to people who haven't heard of you yet. It's a bigger leap, but it can also be a bigger reward if done thoughtfully. As you explore your options, you'll also need to decide whether to keep your business fully under your control or explore franchising. Franchising is a way to scale quickly without having to manage every new location yourself. Instead of opening and operating each spot, you license your brand, systems, and recipes to others who run the new locations. It's a strategy that has worked well for many ramen businesses, but it's not the right choice for everyone.

The biggest advantage of franchising is that it allows you to expand faster while sharing the financial burden with franchisees. Instead of shouldering the full cost of each new location, franchisees invest their own money and take on much of the day-to-day management. This frees you up to focus on growing your brand and refining your systems. However, franchising also means giving up a certain level of control. You'll need to trust that your franchisees will uphold your standards and deliver the same experience that made your first ramen bar successful. If you're considering franchising, take the time to create detailed training programs, operational manuals, and quality control systems. Everything that makes your ramen bar special—your recipes, your service standards, your atmosphere—needs to be documented and repeatable. Franchisees need clear guidance to recreate the magic of your brand in their own locations. You'll also need to carefully vet potential franchisees to ensure they share your vision, values, and commitment to excellence. For some ramen bar owners, keeping it local and fully under their control feels like the better option. Expanding one location at a time allows you to grow more slowly and intentionally, maintaining tight control over every aspect of your business. You can personally train your team, oversee operations, and ensure that each new location lives up to your standards. It's a slower path to growth, but it can also be more sustainable in the long run.

As you consider your options, look to other ramen businesses that have successfully scaled. What can you learn from their experiences? Many of them started small, just like you, with one location and a dream. They expanded thoughtfully, building strong systems, hiring great teams, and staying true to their brand. They didn't rush to grow for the sake of growth they waited until they were truly ready. One lesson many successful ramens bar owners have shared is the importance of staying connected to your customers as you expand. Your first location has a loyal following customer who feel a sense of connection to your restaurant and your story. Don't lose that connection as you grow. Keep engaging with your community, whether it's through social media, events, or simply taking the time to talk to customers when you're in the dining room. That delicate touch is part of what makes your ramen bar special, and it's something that will set you apart even as you scale. Expansion is a big step, and it's not without challenges. There will be days when you wonder if you've bitten off more than you can chew. There will be moments when things go wrong, when a new location doesn't perform as well as you hoped, or when you feel stretched thin. That's normal. Growth is rarely easy, but it's also where the most rewarding moments happen. It's where you prove to yourself that you can take what you've built and make it even bigger, even better. From responding to changing customer preferences to incorporating sustainability into your business model, we'll explore how to keep your ramen bar ahead of the curve. For now, take a moment to reflect on where you started and where you're headed. Expansion is the next chapter in your story, and with the right preparation, it can be the most exciting one yet.

THRIVING THROUGH TRENDS

Running a ramen bar is about so much more than serving bowls of perfect noodles and broth. It's about staying connected to your customers and responding to their evolving tastes and needs. The food industry is constantly shifting. Diets, trends, and customer preferences are like waves always moving, always changing. To thrive, you need to be adaptable, curious, and willing to embrace innovative ideas without losing what makes your ramen bar special. This chapter is about helping you navigate those changes, whether it's creating vegan or gluten-free options, incorporating sustainable practices, or staying ahead of market demands. Dietary trends are no longer niche they're mainstream. Vegan, gluten-free, keto, low-carb these are not passing fads but shifts in the way people think about food. You might be wondering how to cater to these trends without compromising the soul of your ramen. Ramen has its roots in tradition, and the thought of removing pork bones from a rich tonkotsu broth might feel unthinkable. The key is not to view dietary trends as restrictions but as opportunities for creativity and growth. Think about your vegan customers. They still want comfort, flavor, and that satisfying slurp of noodles, just without animal products. Creating a great vegan ramen isn't about simply leaving the meat out it's about reimagining the bowl. Your broth can still be rich and umami-packed with the right ingredients. Kombu, shiitake mushrooms, and miso paste can create a depth of flavor that rivals even the most luxurious pork bone broth. Add toppings like marinated tofu, roasted vegetables, or nori to give the bowl texture and visual appeal. Vegan ramen done well doesn't feel like a compromise; it feels like an experience all its own. For your gluten-free customers, the challenge lies in the noodles. Traditional ramen noodles are made from wheat flour, but there are plenty of high-quality gluten-free alternatives available. Rice noodles, buckwheat soba, or even innovative gluten-free ramen noodles can serve as excellent substitutes. If you decide to offer gluten-free options, make sure you're careful about cross-contamination. Separate cooking pots, utensils, and prep areas are necessary to keep your gluten-free customers safe and confident in their choices.

Keto and low-carb diners present a different challenge. They're often looking for ways to enjoy your ramen without the carb-heavy noodles. You might offer an option to swap noodles for spiralized zucchini, shirataki noodles, or even hearty vegetables like bok choy or cabbage. A rich broth, loaded with protein like chashu pork or chicken, can turn a keto-friendly ramen into a satisfying and flavorful meal. The point isn't to cater to every single dietary preference on the planet it's to show your customers that you're willing to adapt, listen, and find creative ways to make everyone feel welcome. Adapting to trends doesn't mean sacrificing your identity. You don't have to change your entire menu to meet every dietary need. What you're doing is creating options. You're giving customers who might otherwise feel left out a reason to visit your ramen bar and experience what you have to offer. One or two thoughtfully crafted dishes that meet those dietary needs can go a long way in building trust and loyalty.

As you adapt to trends, consider how you can incorporate sustainability into your business model. Sustainability is more than a buzzword. It's about making choices that are better for the environment, your community, and your bottom line. Customers today care about where their food comes from, how it's made, and the impact it has on the planet. By embracing sustainability, you're not only appealing to their values you're setting yourself apart as a business that cares. Start with your ingredients. Where do they come from? Can you source more of your ingredients locally to reduce your carbon footprint and support nearby farmers? Local produce often tastes better because it's fresher, and it tells a story that your customers will appreciate. Imagine serving a bowl of ramen with vegetables sourced from a farm just a few miles away or highlighting locally raised pork in your chashu. These choices add meaning to your food. Reducing food waste is another way to make your ramen bar more sustainable. Broth, for example, is an incredible opportunity to use ingredients efficiently. Bones, vegetable scraps, and kombu can be simmered for hours to create flavor-packed broths that minimize waste. Train your kitchen team to use ingredients thoughtfully and find creative ways to repurpose leftovers. Even small steps like offering smaller portion sizes or letting customers take home leftovers in eco-friendly containers can make an enormous difference. Speaking of eco-friendly containers, take a close look at your packaging, especially if you're offering takeout and delivery. Plastic containers might be cheap and convenient, but they're also one of the biggest contributors to environmental waste. Compostable bowls, biodegradable utensils, and recyclable packaging show your customers that you care about sustainability. Yes, these options might cost a little more, but many customers are willing to pay a slight premium for a business that aligns with their values. Sustainability can also extend to how you run your restaurant. Are you using energy-efficient equipment? Are you reducing water waste in your kitchen? Even simple actions, like switching to LED lighting or offering reusable chopsticks and dishes for dine-in guests, can make a noticeable impact. When you incorporate sustainability into your business, you're not just making responsible choices you're showing your customers that you're thinking about the bigger picture.

Staying ahead of market demands requires a balance of awareness and intuition. Trends will come and go, but the best way to stay relevant is to stay curious. Pay attention to what your customers are asking for, what other restaurants are doing, and what's happening in the broader food industry. Are plant-based dishes becoming more popular? Are people craving bold, spicy flavors? Are comfort foods making a comeback? The more you listen and observe, the better you'll be at anticipating what your customers want. Staying adaptable doesn't mean chasing every trend. You don't have to jump on every bandwagon just because it's popular. Focus on trends that align with your brand and vision. If you've built your reputation on authentic, traditional ramen, then a vegan miso ramen makes sense because it still feels true to who you are. If your style leans toward bold, fusion flavors, then experimenting with new ingredients and techniques might be the right move. The key is to evolve without losing yourself. Your ability to adapt to trends, incorporate sustainability, and meet changing demands is what will keep your ramen bar alive and thriving. Customers want to support businesses that care about their needs, their values, and the future. By staying connected to your community and keeping an open mind, you'll be able to navigate whatever changes come your way. Whether it's an economic downturn, a supply chain issue, or a global crisis, you'll learn how to build a resilient ramen bar that can survive and thrive no matter what comes your way. For now, embrace the changes around you. Your willingness to adapt is what will set you apart and carry you forward.

PART 5: SUSTAINING THE DREAM

Weathering the Storm

Running a ramen bar is a labor of love. You've poured your heart into the broth, fine-tuned every detail of your menu, and built a space where people feel at home. The crowds have come, the bowls are being slurped clean, and it feels like you're living the dream. But there's always a part of you that worries—what happens when things get hard? What happens when the economy dips, the supply chain stumbles, or a crisis comes out of nowhere and blindsides your business? That fear is natural. Every restaurant owner feels it, even the ones who look like they have everything figured out. You've already overcome so much to get to this point, and here's the truth: you can handle what comes next. Success in this business isn't just about good food and happy customers. It's about resilience. It's about preparing for challenges before they happen and building a business that's strong enough to weather any storm. This chapter is about helping you do just that—preparing for economic downturns, managing unexpected crises, and creating a financial safety net to keep your ramen bar alive no matter what comes your way. Economic downturns are part of life, and the food industry often feels them faster and harder than most. When people tighten their belts, dining out is one of the first things to go. You might notice fewer customers coming in, smaller orders, or a drop in regular traffic. It's scary to see those numbers dip, especially when you're used to a full dining room. The key to surviving an economic slowdown is to plan and stay adaptable. Start by looking at your expenses. Where can you reduce costs without sacrificing quality or the customer experience? You streamline your menu, focusing on your best-selling, most profitable dishes. This not only helps you save on inventory but also simplifies operations for your team. Pay attention to portion sizes and food waste—every dollar saved on ingredients is a dollar that can help you get through the lean times. At the same time, think about ways to encourage customers to keep coming in, even when budgets are tight. Small promotions can make a significant difference—things like happy hour specials, combo meals, or loyalty rewards for frequent diners. You don't need to give everything away for free, but you do need to show your customers that you understand their situation and want to make it easier for them to enjoy your food. A small incentive, like a discounted appetizer or a free topping upgrade, can make people feel valued and appreciated.

Diversifying your revenue streams can also help you stay afloat during tough times. If foot traffic slows down, can you boost delivery and takeout sales? Are there catering opportunities or meal kits you can offer to reach customers who are staying home? By spreading your income across different channels, you're less vulnerable to fluctuations in any one area. The key is to stay flexible and open to innovative ideas. Economic downturns force you to get creative, but sometimes those challenges lead to your best solutions. Managing unexpected crises requires a similar mindset—preparation, adaptability, and clear communication. No one could have predicted the way the food industry was turned upside down during the pandemic. Restaurants closed overnight, supply chains crumbled, and owners had to pivot just to survive. It was a brutal reminder that no matter how well you plan, crises will happen. The question is not if, but when—and how you'll respond.

The first step in managing any crisis is staying calm. When you're faced with a challenge—whether it's a sudden supply shortage, a piece of broken equipment, or a situation as massive as a pandemic—it's easy to feel overwhelmed. Take a moment to breathe and assess the situation. What's the immediate problem, and what steps can you take right now to address it? Break the crisis into smaller pieces so it feels more manageable. If your supplier can't deliver a key ingredient, for example, start by looking for alternative sources or temporarily adjusting your menu. Clear, honest communication is critical during any crisis. Your customers and your team will look to you for leadership, and it's important to keep them informed. If your hours are changing, if you're offering new services like takeout or delivery, or if there's a delay in orders, be upfront about it. Customers are more understanding than you might think, especially when they see that you're doing your best under difficult circumstances. Use social media, your website, and signage in your restaurant to keep everyone updated. Your team is your greatest asset during a crisis, so take care of them. Check in with your staff regularly and let them know you appreciate their hard work. If hours need to be cut or roles need to shift, be transparent about why it's happening and what you're doing to keep the business afloat. A strong, motivated team will help you weather the storm more effectively than anything else.

Building a financial safety net is one of the smartest things you can do to prepare for unexpected challenges. It's not easy, especially when you're putting so much into running your restaurant but having a safety net can be the difference between surviving a crisis and closing your doors. Start by creating a savings plan for your business. Even small, consistent contributions to an emergency fund can add up over time. Aim to set aside enough to cover at least a few months' worth of operating expenses—rent, payroll, utilities, and inventory. In addition to savings, explore other financial tools that can help you stay afloat during tough times. A line of credit or a small business loan can provide a cushion when cash flow slows down. Just be cautious about taking on too much debt—borrow only what you need and have a clear plan for how you'll repay it. Knowing that you have options can provide peace of mind and give you the confidence to face challenges head-on. There's also value in building strong relationships with your suppliers, landlords, and financial partners before a crisis hits. If you've built trust and proven yourself reliable, they'll be more likely to work with you when times get tough. Your supplier can offer a payment plan, or your landlord can provide temporary rent relief. These relationships are built on communication, honesty, and mutual respect—things that take time to cultivate but pay off when you need them most.

Resilience is what will keep your ramen bar alive through the difficulties. It's not about avoiding challenges—it's about preparing for them, adapting when they happen, and finding strength in yourself and your team. Challenges will come. Some will be small, like a piece of equipment breaking during a busy shift. Others will feel monumental, like a sudden drop in sales or an unexpected closure. Each one will test you, but each one will also teach you something. You've already proven that you have what it takes to bring your vision to life. You've faced fears, overcome doubts, and built something amazing. That same grit and determination will carry you through whatever comes next. The key is to stay focused on what you can control. You can't stop an economic downturn, but you can control how you respond to it. You can't predict a crisis, but you can prepare for one. In the next chapter, we'll talk about the power of feedback and continuous improvement. You'll learn how to gather insights from your customers, your team, and your own experiences to keep your ramen bar growing.

FEEDBACK FUELS GROWTH

The moment you opened your ramen bar, you entered into a quiet but unspoken agreement with your customers: you serve them the best ramen you can, and in return, they share their honest experience. Whether it's through their words, their actions, or their silence, every customer is telling you something about your business. Their feedback—spoken and unspoken—is one of the most powerful tools you must improve, grow, and thrive. This chapter is about helping you truly listen to that feedback, analyze it, and use it to make your ramen bar even better. It's about turning your customers into your greatest teachers and fostering a culture of continuous improvement that keeps you ahead of the curve. Gathering feedback starts with being intentional. It's easy to assume that no news is good news—that if your customers aren't complaining, everything must be fine. But silence doesn't always mean satisfaction. Someone didn't love their ramen, but they didn't feel comfortable saying so. Someone was frustrated by the wait time, but they didn't think it was worth mentioning. Unspoken feedback is like a whisper you can barely hear, but it holds valuable lessons if you know how to tune into it. The first step is creating opportunities for customers to share their thoughts. Start with the simplest, most immediate method: talking to them. Train your servers to engage with customers in a way that feels natural, not forced. A quick, "How was everything for you today?" as plates are cleared, or checks are dropped can open the door to honest feedback. If a customer hesitates or gives a lukewarm response, encourage your team to dig a little deeper. "Is there anything we could have done to make it better?" Most people appreciate being asked, if it feels sincere.

Online reviews are another invaluable source of feedback. Yelp, Google, Facebook—these platforms are where customers share what they loved and what they didn't. Reading reviews can be humbling, even painful, but they're an unfiltered window into your customers' experiences. Look for patterns. Are multiple people saying the same thing about your broth, your service, or your prices? A single comment might be an outlier, but repeated feedback points to a real issue—or a real strength. Don't just read reviews; engage with them. Thank customers for their positive feedback and respond thoughtfully to negative ones. Avoid canned responses—people can spot insincerity a mile away. Instead, take the time to address their concerns directly. If someone had an unpleasant experience, acknowledge it, apologize sincerely, and offer to make it right. You invite them back for a free bowl, or you explain how you've addressed the problem. A customer who feels heard is more likely to give you another chance, and anyone reading your response will see that you care about your guests. Beyond reviews, consider implementing systems to gather structured feedback. Comment cards at the table, follow-up emails after an online order, or QR codes that lead to quick surveys can give customers an uncomplicated way to share their thoughts. Keep your questions focused and simple. "How was your meal today?" "What did you love?" "What could we improve?" Avoid making the process feel like a chore. People are more likely to respond if it's quick, easy, and respectful of their time.

Once you've gathered feedback, the real work begins analyzing it. Feedback is only valuable if you know how to use it. Look for trends across multiple sources—conversations, reviews, comment cards, and social media. Customers keep mentioning that your broth is too salty, or they love the flavor but wish it were spicier. They rave about your noodles but feel the wait times are too long during peak hours. These insights are like pieces of a puzzle, and your job is to put them together to see the full picture. Not all feedback is created equal. Learning to filter the noise is just as important as listening. Some comments will be vague or unhelpful—like someone saying, "It was fine" without elaborating. Others might be overly critical or unrealistic. Someone complains about your prices but doesn't understand the quality of your ingredients. Take a step back and evaluate each piece of feedback in context. If a comment aligns with patterns you're seeing elsewhere, it's worth addressing. If it feels isolated or unreasonable, don't let it shake your confidence. Use the insights you gather to make meaningful improvements to your operations and offerings. Start small. If customers consistently say they want more topping options, experiment with adding a few new choices. If they're frustrated by long wait times, look at ways to streamline your service—maybe it's time to add another server during peak hours or optimize how orders flow to the kitchen. The changes don't need to be drastic, but they do need to show customers that you're listening.

Continuous improvement is a mindset, not a one-time effort. It's about creating a culture where you're always looking for ways to be better, even when things are going well. Share feedback with your team regularly—both the good and the bad—and involve them in finding solutions. If a customer mentions that a server went beyond, celebrate it. Recognize the team member in front of everyone and highlight what made the experience special. Positive reinforcement motivates your team to keep delivering exceptional service.

At the same time, use constructive feedback as a learning opportunity. If a customer felt neglected during their meal, don't point fingers. Instead, ask, "What could we do differently next time?" Encourage your team to view feedback as a tool for growth, not a personal attack. When everyone feels like they're part of the solution, they'll take more ownership of their roles and responsibilities. Improving your offerings based on feedback can also help you stay ahead of customer expectations. Customers keep asking for a vegetarian ramen that's as flavorful as your pork-based bowls. Use that feedback as inspiration to create something incredible. People love your tonkotsu but wish it were available in a smaller portion for lunch. Small tweaks like this show your customers that you're paying attention to their needs and constantly striving to serve them better. Feedback also has a way of shining a light on your strengths. It's easy to focus on the criticisms, but don't ignore the praise. If customers consistently rave about your spicy miso ramen or your perfectly soft-boiled eggs, lean into that. Highlight those dishes on your menu, feature them on social media, and make them a signature part of your brand. Your strengths are what set you apart, and feedback helps you recognize them. Gathering and analyzing feedback isn't just about fixing problems; it's about building relationships. When customers see that their voices matter, they become more invested in your restaurant. They go from being occasional diners to loyal regulars, from silent visitors to vocal advocates. They'll tell their friends, leave glowing reviews, and keep coming back because they know you care about their experience.

As you grow, feedback will remain your compass. It will guide you through tough decisions, inspire latest ideas, and help you stay connected to the people you serve. Running a ramen bar is an ongoing journey of learning, adapting, and improving. Each bowl you serve, each conversation you have, and each review you read is a chance to get better. In the next chapter, we'll talk about building your legacy—how to share your story, inspire others, and leave a lasting impact on your community and the industry. For now, focus on listening. Your customers are telling you everything you need to know to keep growing, thriving, and serving ramen that makes them feel at home.

THE RAMEN LEGACY

There's something no one tells you when you're chasing a dream: it's easy to lose yourself in the process. Owning a ramen bar, or any business for that matter, has a way of becoming all-consuming. It starts with the best of intentions late nights, early mornings, and skipped meals because there's "just one more thing" to do. You pour your energy, your heart, and your soul into every detail, and before you know it, the dream that once lit you up starts to feel like it's burning you out. This chapter is about finding balance. It's about making sure you don't lose yourself in the work. It's about stepping back to embrace the journey and learning the lessons that only come from pursuing your passion. Hana knew this better than anyone. When she first opened her ramen bar, she did everything. She was the first to arrive and the last to leave. She chopped vegetables, cooked broth, greeted customers, and handled the books after hours. Her restaurant was her life, and in those early months, it felt like she couldn't step away for even a minute. Every time she thought about taking a day off, her mind would swirl with a thousand worries. What if something went wrong? What if a customer had an unpleasant experience? What if the broth wasn't perfect? It took a conversation with an old friend for Hana to realize she was running on empty. One evening, after yet another 16-hour day, she sat down across from her friend, who quietly asked, "Why did you open this place?" Hana blinked, confused. "To share something I love," she answered. "To make people happy." Her friend smiled gently and said, "And are you happy?" The question hit Hana like a freight train. She loved her ramen bar—she truly did—but she hadn't given herself permission to enjoy it. She was so focused on keeping the dream alive that she hadn't realized she was letting herself disappear in the process.

Balance isn't just a buzzword; it's a survival strategy. Your ramen bar needs you at your best, and you can't give your best when you're exhausted, overwhelmed, or burned out. It's easy to convince yourself that you must do everything, especially in the beginning. You tell yourself that no one else will care as much as you do, or that stepping back means you're not committed. The truth is, letting go of that mindset is one of the most powerful things you can do—for yourself, for your team, and for your business. Start by recognizing that balance isn't about perfection. There will be weeks when the restaurant demands more of you, and that's okay. Balance isn't a fixed state—it's a constant recalibration. It's about making sure that, over time, you're prioritizing your health, your relationships, and your happiness just as much as you're prioritizing your business. You are not your ramen bar. You are a person with a life, with dreams, with people who love you, and it's okay to step away sometimes. Delegate, trust, and empower your team. If you've hired the right people and trained them well, they can handle more than you think. Give them the responsibility and trust to run the restaurant without you hovering over their shoulders. Let your head chef take ownership of the kitchen and let your front-of-house manager handle the dining room. Allowing your team to shine not only gives you room to breathe but also helps them feel invested in the success of the business.

Find time to reconnect with the things that light you up outside of work. It's spending an afternoon with family, getting back into a hobby you've neglected, or simply taking a quiet moment to breathe. Hana started scheduling small breaks for herself—an afternoon off here, a morning to sleep in there. At first, it felt uncomfortable, like she was abandoning her restaurant. But something amazing happened. When she returned, she felt sharper, more focused, and more energized. The space she gave herself allowed her to show up for her customers and her team in a better way. Owning a ramen bar is about the journey, not just the destination. It's easy to get so caught up in chasing the next milestone more customers, higher profits, a second location—that you forget to appreciate where you are right now. Take a moment to look around. Think about the first day you unlocked the door to your restaurant. Think about the smell of that first pot of broth simmering on the stove. Think about the first time a customer told you they'd never tasted anything so good. Those moments matter. Hana learned to celebrate the small victories. A record-breaking Friday night. A glowing review from a customer. A new dish that quickly became a crowd favorite. She started keeping a journal, writing down moments of gratitude and pride at the end of each week. It was her way of reminding herself why she started and how far she'd come. Every time the doubts crept in, or the workload felt overwhelming, she'd flip back through her notes and see the proof of her progress.

The truth is, running a restaurant will teach you more about yourself than you ever imagined. You'll learn how to face fear and uncertainty head-on. You'll learn how to trust others and let go of control. You'll learn how to keep moving forward, even when it feels like the odds are stacked against you. Most importantly, you'll learn that success isn't just about the ramen bar you build—it's about the person you become in the process. You will make mistakes. You will have days when you wonder why you ever thought this was an innovative idea. You'll have moments when the kitchen is chaos, a customer complaint, or a piece of equipment breaks at the worst possible time. Those moments will test you, but they will also teach you. Every challenge you overcome will make you stronger, more resilient, and more capable than you were before.

Hana often said that her ramen bar was her greatest teacher. It taught her patience when things didn't happen as quickly as she wanted. It taught her humility when she realized she couldn't do it all alone. It taught her to embrace the uncertainty and trust the process, even when she couldn't see the path ahead clearly. The lessons she learned in the kitchen and the dining room spilled over into every part of her life, shaping her into someone she was proud to be. As you continue this journey, remember to give yourself grace. You are not striving for perfection; you are striving for progress. The ramen bar you're building reflects your passion, your creativity, and your willingness to keep showing up, no matter what. It's a reflection of your heart, and that's something no challenge can take away. In the next chapter, we'll talk about celebrating your success and building a legacy that lasts. You've come so far, and there's still so much ahead of you. For now, take a deep breath and remind yourself of this: you're not just building a restaurant; you're building a life. Embrace the journey. It's yours, and it's worth every step.

PERSONAL GROWTH THROUGH RAMEN

Owning a ramen bar can be one of the most rewarding experiences of your life, but let's be real—it's also one of the hardest. No one tells you how all-encompassing it becomes. It's not just a job. It's not even just a dream. It's your identity. It feels like the lifeblood of who you are, and because of that, it can swallow everything else if you let it. You're up at dawn thinking about inventory. You're running to the restaurant before the first delivery truck arrives. You're there long after the last table has been wiped down, worrying about tomorrow's prep. You're always planning, always tweaking, always trying to solve the next problem before it even happens. It feels like there's no off switch. Even when you're home, your mind drifts back to the restaurant. You think about that new dish you want to try. You wonder if the new server is picking things up fast enough. You run through numbers in your head, trying to decide if you can afford a bigger noodle cooker or a second delivery driver. At night, you dream about ramen broth, noodles, toppings like your subconscious refuses to clock out. That's what happens when you care this much. The line between your work and your life starts to blur until you can't see it anymore. And then one day, you look up and realize you haven't seen your friends in weeks. You can't remember the last time you had a real day off, one where you didn't answer a single work email or phone call. You missed an important event a family gathering, a birthday dinner, something you swore you wouldn't skip but the restaurant had "just one more thing" that needed your attention. The guilt starts to creep in. You feel like you're sacrificing parts of yourself, and at the same time, you wonder if you're doing enough. It's exhausting.

Here's the truth no one tells you: finding balance doesn't mean caring less about your dream. It doesn't mean stepping away or letting someone else take over what you've built. Balance means learning to take care of yourself with the same energy, intention, and care that you put into your ramen bar. Because without you—without your heart, your vision, and your presence there is no ramen bar. It can't thrive if you're running on empty. The only way your dream survives long-term is if you do, too. Start by setting boundaries. I know, it sounds impossible. How do you walk away when the restaurant needs you? But here's the thing: it will always need you. There will always be something that feels urgent. You could work 24 hours a day and still find a task undone. Boundaries aren't about abandoning the work; they're about protecting your energy so you can keep showing up for it. Decide on small, realistic steps to take back your time. It's leaving the restaurant at a specific time every night and trusting your team to close without you. It's committing to taking one full day off every week no emails, no calls, no sneaking back to check on things. Balance starts with trust. You must trust your team to carry the load when you're not there. I know how hard that is. No one else cares as much as you do, right? That's the lie we tell ourselves, and it's what keeps us trapped in a cycle of overwork. The truth is, when you empower your team when you train them, trust them, and let them take ownership they step up. They take pride in the restaurant, too. Give them room to handle things without you hovering over their shoulder. You'll be amazed at what they're capable of.

Finding balance also means reconnecting with the things that make you feel alive outside of work. Remember who you were before the ramen bar. What did you love to do? Who did you love to spend time with? It's okay to step away for an afternoon to go hiking, to take a pottery class, to sit at home with a good book. It's not wasted time. It's time that fills your cup so you can pour into your work again. You don't have to feel guilty for taking care of yourself. The journey of owning a ramen bar isn't about racing to the finish line. It's not about hitting a specific profit number or expanding to a second location or becoming the most popular spot in town though those milestones might happen along the way. It's about embracing the process, the work, and the growth that happens as you move forward. Every day brings a lesson, even when it doesn't feel like it. Especially when it doesn't feel like it. Some days will feel like victories the nights when the line stretches out the door, the moments when a customer tells you it's the best meal they've ever had, the days when everything just clicks. Other days will humble you. The food shipment that shows up late. The equipment that breaks in the middle of dinner service. The customer who leaves an unfair review online. It's in those moments that you grow the most, because you learn how to adapt, how to persevere, and how to stay focused on what matters.

Running your ramen bar will teach you patience. You'll learn that success doesn't happen overnight. It's built slowly, one bowl at a time, one customer at a time, one day at a time. It will teach you humility. You'll realize that you can't do it all on your own and that you don't have all the answers, and that's okay. It will teach you gratitude. For the quiet mornings before service starts. For the loyal customers who keep showing up. For the team that stands by your side, even on the toughest days. Most of all, it will teach you resilience. There will be days when you feel like giving up, when the weight of the work feels too heavy. You'll question yourself. You'll wonder if you made the right choice, if you're strong enough to keep going. And then you'll remember why you started. You'll remember that first spark of excitement, the moment you knew you wanted to open your ramen bar. You'll remember the love and passion that brought you here. That's what keeps you going. The lessons you learn from pursuing your passion don't stay within the walls of your restaurant. They follow you everywhere. They change the way you approach challenges, the way you build relationships, and the way you see yourself. You become someone who knows how to dream big, work hard, and adapt when things don't go as planned. You become someone who doesn't give up. Owning a ramen bar isn't just about serving food. It's about creating experiences, building community, and sharing a piece of yourself with the world. It's about the journey every messy, beautiful, exhausting step of it. The late nights and early mornings. The triumphs and the setbacks. The days when you want to throw in the towel and the moments when you can't believe how far you've come. It's all part of the story you're writing, one day at a time. It's something you create every day. You're doing better than you think, and you're stronger than you know. Keep going there's so much more ahead of you.

YOUR BOWL, YOUR LEGACY

You've made it. Take a moment to let that sink in. Everything you've been through—every long night, every early morning, every hard decision—has brought you here. Your ramen bar isn't just a dream anymore; it's real. It's a place where people gather, a place where your passion lives in every bowl, and a place where you've built something that matters. If you look back at where you started, it might seem like a lifetime ago. You were just a person with an idea, a little fire of hope in your chest, and a willingness to take a risk. Now you've built something that exists in the real world. That's no small thing. The journey hasn't been perfect, and it hasn't always been easy, but that's what makes it meaningful. Every milestone you've hit along the way deserves to be celebrated. It was your first day with a packed house, the kind of night where the energy buzzed, and you couldn't wipe the smile off your face even as you raced to keep up with orders. It was the first time you got a glowing review online, or the day someone told you your ramen reminded them of home. It was the moment you hired your first full-time employee, or when you finally turned a profit after months of grinding it out. Each of these moments is a victory, no matter how big or small. They're proof of how far you've come and how much you've accomplished. Take time to acknowledge those milestones, not just for yourself but for your team and your community. You're not on this journey alone. Your staff has been there through the chaos and the calm, the highs and the lows, giving their time, energy, and talent to make your ramen bar what it is today. Celebrate them. A team dinner, a heartfelt thank-you speech, or even just a quiet moment to say, "I see you. I appreciate you." These gestures matter more than you know. Your customers have been part of the story, too. Whether it's your regulars who show up every week or the people who spread the word to their friends and family, they're the ones who've kept you going. Celebrate with them. A customer appreciation night, a special giveaway, or a simple thank-you note can make them feel like they're part of something bigger.

As you celebrate your success, it's natural to start thinking about what comes next. You've built something incredible, and now it's time to plan for the future. You're ready to expand, opening a second location or creating new ventures that build on the brand you've already created. You're thinking about stepping back someday, handing the reins to someone you trust so you can focus on new dreams or finally take a well-earned rest. Succession planning isn't about giving up your legacy; it's about making sure it lives on. Start by thinking about what you want the future to look like. If you're planning to pass your ramen bar down to a family member, a trusted employee, or even a partner, take the time to prepare them. Teach them the systems, the recipes, and the values that have made your ramen bar a success. Share your stories, your lessons, and your vision. Make sure they understand not just how the restaurant runs but why it exists in the first place. Your legacy isn't just about the food—it's about the care, the creativity, and the culture you've built. That's what will carry it forward.

You're ready to take a step back and let retirement become part of the plan. Retirement doesn't mean walking away from everything you've built. It means stepping into a new season of your life, knowing that your hard work has created something that can stand on its own. You can still be part of the story, offering guidance when it's needed or showing up to enjoy a bowl of ramen in the dining room like any other guest. You've earned that. For some, the future means exploring new ventures—opening a different kind of restaurant, launching a product line, or mentoring the next generation of ramen entrepreneurs. You've been dreaming about creating your own brand of noodles or a line of ready-to-serve broths. You're ready to write your own cookbook or teach workshops that inspire others to follow their dreams. Your experience has value, and there's no limit to the ways you can share it with the world. No matter what the future holds, remember that your ramen bar is more than just a business. It's your legacy. It's the lives you've touched, the relationships you've built, and the impact you've made on your community. It's the family who comes in every Sunday night for their favorite bowl. It's the student who treats themselves to a steaming bowl after a long day of classes. It's the couple who shares their first date at your restaurant and comes back years later to celebrate an anniversary. These are the stories you've helped create, and they're part of what makes your ramen bar unforgettable. The impact you leave doesn't stop at your customers. Your ramen bar is part of something bigger—your neighborhood, your city, your industry. You've inspired other local businesses to follow their own dreams, or maybe you've helped put your community on the map as a food destination. Your work has ripples, even if you don't always see them. Think about the industry itself. You're part of a tradition that stretches across generations and cultures, a tradition that continues to evolve because of people like you—people who care deeply, work tirelessly, and take risks to share their vision. You've left your mark on that tradition, adding your own voice, your own flavors, and your own story to the world of ramen. That's something to be proud of.

As this journey comes full circle, there's one more thing to remember: your story doesn't have to end here. There will always be new dreams to chase, new lessons to learn, and new people to inspire. Your ramen bar is a testament to what's possible when you follow your passion, and now it's time to share that story with others. You know someone who's dreaming of opening their own restaurant but doesn't know where to start. A friend has mentioned a passion they've been too afraid to pursue. Share what you've learned. Encourage them to take the first step. Let them know that if you can do it, they can, too. Your journey can inspire others to chase their own dreams. Whether it's opening a ramen bar, starting a bakery, or launching a food truck, the lessons you've learned apply to anyone with a dream and a willingness to work for it. Share this book, share your experiences, and remind the people around you that their passion is worth pursuing. Sometimes all it takes is a little nudge—someone to say, "I believe in you." Be that nudge.

As you turn the page on this chapter of your life, take a moment to appreciate what you've built. It's more than a restaurant. It's a legacy of hard work, creativity, and heart. It's a reminder that dreams are worth chasing, even when the path is uncertain. Your ramen bar is proof that with vision, determination, and love, you can create something that changes lives—yours included.

This is your story. Your bowls of ramen have nourished more than just hungry stomachs—they've nourished connections, communities, and dreams. That's a legacy worth celebrating.

The next chapter is yours to write, and it starts with sharing this story. Pass it along to anyone who needs it. Anyone who's ever dreamed of opening a ramen bar or any restaurant. Anyone who's been afraid to take the leap. Remind them that every great journey starts with a single step, and they already have everything they need to begin.

Thank you for letting me be part of this story. Now it's your turn to inspire the next one.

FREE RECIPES YOU MAY ENJOY!

Spicy Miso Curry Ramen

I want you to picture this bowl in front of you. The broth is deep orange, almost glowing. It's creamy but has a bite to it, a warmth that hits the back of your throat and lingers just long enough. This is the kind of ramen you make when you want people to stop mid-bite and say, "Wow." I remember the first time I tasted something like this. It was on a rainy day, and I stumbled into a tiny ramen shop that barely had enough seats for six people. The chef handed me a steaming bowl, and the smell alone knocked me back—a mix of miso, curry spice, and chili oil that curled up from the broth like a warm invitation. I didn't know ramen could taste like that. It felt familiar and exciting all at once, like comfort food with a punch of rebellion.

Start with the broth. Use a base of chicken stock or vegetable broth, simmering it until it's rich and balanced. Stir in white miso paste, letting it dissolve slowly, then add a spoonful of Japanese curry powder. That's where the magic starts to happen—the miso gives it depth, and the curry adds a warmth that sneaks up on you. To make it creamy, add a swirl of coconut milk toward the end. Let it simmer, low and slow, until it tastes like something that could heal any bad day. The toppings are where you take this bowl over the top. Brown some ground pork in a pan, adding garlic, ginger, and a sprinkle of curry powder to tie it all together. Spoon it generously over the noodles. Then, add a soft-boiled egg —perfectly jammy—and charred corn that's been kissed by fire.

Finally, a drizzle of chili oil brings it all home. Serve it with thick, chewy noodles that hold onto the broth like they never want to let go. This is the bowl that warms you from the inside out, the one people will order again and again because they can't stop thinking about it.

RUFFLE SHOYU RAMEN

If you've ever wanted to make ramen that feels like a special occasion—something luxurious but approachable—this is the bowl. I first tasted truffle ramen in a small shop in Tokyo, tucked into a quiet alleyway. The shop was unassuming, but the ramen felt like art. It was delicate and simple, but then there was this something extra, an earthy aroma that lingered with every bite. I found out later it was truffle oil, just a few drops stirred into the broth at the very end. It transformed the entire bowl.

This starts with a clear, clean shoyu broth—a mix of soy sauce, dashi, and chicken stock. Simmer it gently, respecting the simplicity of the ingredients. When it's ready, you'll know because the aroma will fill your kitchen like a promise.

To bring this bowl to life, you need the right toppings. Seared shiitake mushrooms add an umami punch that pairs beautifully with the broth. If you want to elevate it further, top it with roasted duck breast or pork belly that's been crisped on the edges. Before serving, stir a few drops of truffle oil into the broth. It doesn't need much. That's the beauty of it. Finish the bowl with microgreens and a soft-boiled egg sprinkled with truffle salt. This is the kind of ramen that makes people close their eyes and savor every bite, like they're tasting something rare and precious.

VEGAN COCONUT LEMONGRASS RAMEN

I'm going to tell you something about this bowl—it's pure joy. The kind of ramen you make when you want to feel refreshed and inspired. I created a version of this after a long summer trip through Southeast Asia, where every meal seemed to smell of lemongrass, ginger, and lime. It's bright, it's creamy, and it somehow feels both light and rich at the same time. Perfect for the customer who says, "I don't eat meat, but I still want something incredible."

Start with a base of coconut milk and vegetable stock. Add bruised lemongrass stalks, fresh ginger, and kaffir lime leaves, letting them simmer until the broth is fragrant and alive. This broth doesn't need hours on the stove. It comes together quickly, but every spoonful feels intentional. The toppings are where you let the vegetables shine. Crispy tofu—golden brown on the edges—sits next to charred bok choy and roasted sweet potato. Garnish the bowl with fresh cilantro, a sprinkle of toasted sesame seeds, and a wedge of lime on the side. The first bite should taste like an adventure, bright and creamy, with flavors that dance on the tongue.

SMOKY TONKOTSU RAMEN

Tonkotsu ramen is a labor of love. The kind of broth you spend hours—no, days—perfecting. When you get it right, it's worth every single minute. I remember watching a ramen chef once, his eyes completely focused on a giant pot of simmering pork bones. He stirred it slowly, methodically, like the entire success of his shop depended on it. Maybe it did. Tonkotsu broth is milky, rich, and heavy with depth. Adding a smoky twist takes it to an entirely new level.

Start with a traditional tonkotsu broth. Simmer pork bones for hours until the broth turns creamy and opaque. That's when you know you're onto something special. To give it the smoky edge, you're going to make mayu, a black garlic oil that's deeply rich with flavor. Roast garlic until it's almost black—right at the edge of burning—and blend it with sesame oil until it's glossy and perfect.

Ladle the broth over thin, straight noodles, then top it with thick slices of pork belly that have been lightly charred for a smoky finish. Swirl the black garlic oil into the broth. It pools at the edges, dark and mysterious, ready to be mixed in. Add finely chopped scallions, pickled ginger, and a soft-boiled egg. This is the kind of ramen that feels indulgent, the bowl that makes customers sigh with happiness after their first bite.

KIMCHI AND BUTTER CORN RAMEN

Sometimes the best ideas come when you least expect them. This bowl was inspired by a late-night craving—one of those nights when you throw together what's in the fridge and accidentally create something amazing. I had leftover kimchi, a can of sweet corn, and some chili paste, and what started as a "whatever's here" meal turned into something worth putting on any menu.

The broth starts with chicken or vegetable stock. Stir in a spoonful of gochujang—Korean chili paste—to give it depth and heat. Then add a splash of kimchi juice. It's funky, spicy, and full of personality. Top the noodles with buttered corn that's been sautéed just enough to caramelize slightly. Add a generous spoonful of spicy, fermented kimchi and some ground pork or chicken cooked with garlic and soy sauce. The final touch is a small pat of butter right in the center of the bowl. As it melts, it adds richness to the broth that ties everything together. This is the bowl that surprises people. It's bold, unexpected, and deeply satisfying—like a perfect late-night discovery that somehow makes it onto the main menu.

JOIN THE JOURNEY

Before you move on, let me ask you this: how great would it be to keep the ramen inspiration going even after you turn the last page? By subscribing to the email list, you'll get exclusive updates on future books, fresh restaurant tips, and brand-new recipes to keep your creativity flowing.

Think of it as your next step in this journey. I'll share bonus content you won't find anywhere else—insider stories, ideas to improve your ramen bar, and special recipes you can try before anyone else. You're building something amazing, and I want to help you keep growing long after you finish this book.

It's easy. Head over to subscribepage.io/ChefKatCarter and sign up. Let's keep the ideas simmering, the recipes flowing, and the dream alive. I can't wait to see what you create next.

AFTERWORD

As you turn the last page of this book, I want you to take a moment to reflect on how far you've come. From dreaming about that perfect bowl of ramen to exploring the steps it takes to turn your vision into reality, you've been on a journey—a journey not just of food, but of passion, courage, and discovery. Writing this book was my way of sharing everything I've learned, not just about ramen, but about the power of believing in yourself and building something meaningful.

If there's one thing I hope you take away from this, it's that your dream matters. The ramen bar you've imagined, the bowls you've perfected, the space you want to create—it's all within your reach. Whether you're just starting or already making moves, every step you take brings you closer. There will be challenges, of course, but those challenges are what make the journey worth it. They're what shape you into the kind of person who can bring people together over a bowl of ramen and make them feel at home. I want you to remember that this isn't the end—it's just the beginning. Your story is still being written, one decision, one bowl, one connection at a time. And as you move forward, know that you're not alone. There's a whole community of dreamers and creators, just like you, working to bring something beautiful into the world.

If you've found value in this book, I invite you to stay connected. Join the email list, share your journey, and let's keep growing together. I'll be here, cheering you on, sharing new recipes, tips, and ideas, and celebrating your wins every step of the way.

Thank you for allowing me to be part of your journey. It's been an honor to share this with you, and I can't wait to see what you create. So go out there and make it happen.

ACKNOWLEDGEMENT

This book wouldn't exist without the love, support, and encouragement of so many incredible people. First and foremost, to my family—my husband and our two wonderful children—you are my foundation, my biggest cheerleaders, and the reason I keep dreaming big. Thank you for your patience during long nights of writing, for your endless taste tests, and for always believing in me, even when I doubted myself. I love you more than words can express.

To the countless chefs, food lovers, and entrepreneurs who inspired this journey, thank you for sharing your passion with the world. Your creativity, resilience, and dedication remind me why I love this industry and why I wrote this book. A special thanks to the ramen shop owners who generously opened their doors and shared their stories—they are the heart and soul of this book.

To my mentors, teachers, and friends who guided me along the way, your wisdom has been a lighthouse in moments of uncertainty. Thank you for your advice, your honesty, and your encouragement to push forward, even when the path wasn't clear.

To the readers—this book is for you. Your courage to chase your dreams, your willingness to take risks, and your love for food inspire me more than you'll ever know. I wrote this with the hope that it will help you build something beautiful, not just for yourself but for the communities and lives you'll touch through your work. If you want to continue this journey with me, I invite you to join the email list. By signing up, you'll receive exclusive recipes, behind-the-scenes updates, and tools to take your restaurant ideas even further. Together, we'll keep this momentum going—one step, one bowl, one dream at a time.

    Finally, to the power of ramen itself. It's more than a bowl of food; it's a connection, a memory, and a story. May it continue to bring joy, comfort, and inspiration to all who create and enjoy it.

Thank you from the bottom of my heart,
Chef Kathryn Carter

ABOUT THE AUTHOR

Chef Kathryn Carter

Kathryn Carter is a passionate chef, entrepreneur, and storyteller with a love for both the art of cooking and the business behind it. A proud graduate of Augusta's Culinary School of Colorado, Kathryn has spent years perfecting her craft and exploring the rich and vibrant world of food. Her culinary journey has always been fueled by a deep admiration for ramen—a dish that combines simplicity and complexity in one perfect bowl.

In addition to her culinary expertise, Kathryn holds degrees in Business Management, giving her a unique ability to blend her creative love of food with the strategic know-how to build a thriving restaurant. Her professional background has allowed her to understand not just the flavors that make a dish memorable but also the systems and strategies that make a restaurant successful.

Kathryn's life is full of inspiration. She's happily married to her high school sweetheart and is the proud mom of two wonderful kids, who are often her biggest cheerleaders (and most honest taste-testers). When she's not in the kitchen testing a new broth or dreaming up creative ramen concepts, you can find her enjoying family dinners, exploring food markets, or sharing quiet moments with a cup of coffee and her notebook.

Her love for ramen and small business led her to write this book, a culmination of her experience, passion, and desire to help others bring their own dreams to life. She believes that every great dish tells a story, and every dream deserves a chance to be realized. Through her warm, personal guidance and practical advice, Kathryn hopes to inspire aspiring restaurant owners to take that first step, face every challenge head-on, and create something they can be proud of.

Whether you're an aspiring chef, a food entrepreneur, or simply someone with a big dream, Kathryn's journey—and this book—will show you that with the right blend of passion, hard work, and heart, anything is possible.

www.ingramcontent.com/pod-product-compliance
Lightning Source LLC
Chambersburg PA
CBHW050304230526
45471CB00005B/2014